Heart Warming Truths

To John
from
Drew
April 2015

Heart Warming Truths

Drew Craig

HEART WARMING TRUTHS
By: Drew Craig
Copyright © 2011
GOSPEL FOLIO PRESS
All Rights Reserved

Published by
GOSPEL FOLIO PRESS
304 Killaly St. W.
Port Colborne, ON L3K 6A6
CANADA

ISBN: 9781926765365

Cover design by Lisa Martin

All Scripture quotations from the
King James Version unless otherwise noted.

Printed in USA

Contents

Foreword

Where have six decades gone? Then I was a young Christian learning the Word and ways of God. With many of a like-mind, I was thrilled by the rich ministry of our late brother, Mr. David Craig. Now, with the passing of 60 years, I have the honour of writing the forward to this delightful book from the pen of his son, my friend and brother in Christ, Drew Craig.

The first meditation, "A Caring Creator," captured my attention, and warmed my heart, but that was just the beginning. Every page is exciting and enriching reading, as the author exalts our beloved Lord. He does so as he dwells on "Constraining Love," "God's Pleasure in His Son," who "Demonstrated His Grace." "Moral Excellence" and other great attributes of God and His Son, will encourage you in "Serving Our Own Generation," and "The Kind of People God Uses" — such as "A Man With Fear in His Heart," "A Man with Fountains in His Eyes," "A Man with Fire in His Bones."

Sit back, relax, and meditate on these soul-thrilling themes.

— Arnot McIntee

Introduction

Over recent years since the World Wide Web came into common and universal use I have endeavoured to capture and 'save' devotional and practical teaching from the Scriptures 'on line'. They are really a summary of oral ministry past and present.

What follows is a collation of forty such meditations. They have been listed in alphabetical order but the reader will quickly realise that I have not followed any particular theme. I am hoping that the comparisons and contrasts from one to another will add a sense of spiritual adventure!

The majority are quite brief but I have risked the inclusion of a few more 'meaty' contributions which in content may not fall into line with the convictions of some of my fellow believers. If such is the case I ask for your Christian indulgence.

The dictionary definition of meditation is to be "occupied in thought". The Psalmist articulates this in a number of psalms. Two references will suffice *"Let the words of my mouth and the meditations of my heart be acceptable in thy sight, O Lord, my rock, and my redeemer"* (Psalm 19:14). *"I will sing unto the Lord as long as I live… Let my meditations be sweet unto him: I will rejoice in the Lord"* (Psalm 104:33-34). Our thoughts linked to our hearts affection will lead to a song of thanksgiving and a deeper appreciation of the One who has called us *"out of darkness into his marvellous light"* (1 Pet. 2:9). This is the overall objective of *Heart Warming Thruths.* A title suggested by the publisher.

In conclusion I wish to express my gratitude to my good brother Arnot McIntee for agreeing to write the Foreward. Arnot has spent a lifetime magnifying the Lord Jesus in the proclamation of the Gospel and ministering the Word to the Lord's people in Canada and the USA. I also am grateful to the staff of Gospel Folio Press who have in any way contributed to the production of this publication. They are available, too, as an on going ministry at www.brooklandsgospelcentre.org

—Drew Craig

Dundonald, N. Ireland.

A Caring Creator

"Thou hast granted me life and favour, and thy visitation (care) *hath preserved my spirit"* (Job 10:12).

Job's experience of God reminds me of His attributes: **omnipotence**, **omniscience** and **omnipresence**.

There are many circumstances in our lives where God, unknown to us, has been working with and for us. He has guided, protected and cared for us in the spiritual as well as in the physical areas of our lives.

James reminds us that *"every good and perfect gift cometh down from above from the father of lights with whom there is no variableness"* (Jas. 1:17). Someone has remarked that God's dealings with us are **perfect**, not necessarily **pleasant**!

But in all the variegated experiences of life, the One who created us for His pleasure and redeemed us for His glory *"is working in us both to will and to do of his good pleasure."*

Omnipotence speaks of Authority

Omniscience speaks of Knowledge

Omnipresence speaks of Comfort

Authority, Knowledge and Comfort—what infinite and all embracing resources! Overarching it all, of course, is **love**—the **love** of God.

Could we with ink the ocean fill,

And were the skies of parchment made;

Were every blade of grass a quill,

And every man a scribe by trade;

To write the love of God above,

Would drain the ocean dry;

Nor could the scroll contain the whole
Though stretched from sky to sky.
—Frederick M. Lehman

Some dear soul in discovering the secret of serenity and peace scrawled these precious words on the wall of his prison cell. Yes, this is a God who has invested all that He is and has in us, mere mortals, but destined for immortality. We do not know what lies ahead on our pathway to Heaven, but the care that our God lavishes on us is the deposit for what is yet to be.

John, the apocalyptic seer, has revealed in that coming day of bliss:

"His servants shall serve Him	**Eternally**
They shall see His face	**Literally**
His name shall be on their foreheads"	**Identity**
(Rev. 22:3-4).	

All this puts into context Job's words about **care** and **preservation**!

Babel's Tower

"He made of one every nation of men to dwell on the face of the earth having determined their appointed seasons, and the bounds of their habitation: That they should seek after God" (Acts 17.26-27).

At Babel God scattered mankind and confused their language so that they could not communicate their evil designs to each other. The Apostle told his hearers that God separated the races so that they could concentrate on Him.

Today's consensus is that we need the opposite. The solution to mankind's problems is their regrouping, reuniting and unifying of states. A Lockheed Corporation advertisement showed an illustration of the tower of Babel. Lockheed boasted that its scientific advances were "undoing the Babel effect by bringing mankind together and making it possible to speak one language."

The tower of Babel fills the official poster for the twelve nations of the European Union. Above the unfinished tower circles twelve inverted stars—a symbol of the occult.

International Business Machines (IBM) has also used an artist's depiction of the tower of Babel in some of its advert, with modern high rise buildings protruding from the half finished building.

Soon there will be phones on the market which will allow English to be spoken into the receiver in Los Angeles but heard in Tokyo as Japanese.

Babel's tower stands in stark contrast to the way of salvation which God in His Word has consistently declared from Abel onward. Babel was a continuation of the Adam and Eve rebellion, which separated man from his creator. For man, a finite creature, payment of the infinite penalty demanded by God's justice was impossible. No attempt of man could reconcile himself to God. Man could only drive the wedge of separation further in, as the Babel episode did.

Man's approach to God would be on the basis of an Altar, not a Tower.

By Him And For Him

The way we see our place in the world determines the kind of people we are—having either a wide or a narrow vision. God would have us think in global or strategic terms. To help us do this let us consider:

"And He is before all things and by Him all things consist" (hold together) *"By Him were all things created"* (Col. 1:16-17).

He is the **maker** and **maintainer** of the universe. He is Originator, the Organizer and the One who keeps it in order.

Galaxies in their appointed places.

Planets in their orbits.

Oceans held in their beds,

Rivers running down to the sea,

The mountains and the valleys bearing testimony to Him.

I see in my mind's eye the beautiful Tolleymore Forest Park, here in Northern Ireland. As you leave it there is a message inscribed in a large rock. It reads:

Stop, look around and praise
the name of Him who made it all.

The Hebrews writer, continuing this theme, says that *"he upholds all things by the word of his power"* (Heb. 1:3).

Not an Atlas kind of God, who 'has the whole world in His hands', but rather that He maintains it and moves it along to an ultimate and predestined goal. Scientists tell us that the world's energy is running out. The Scripture states clearly that it will *"wax old as a garment"* (Heb. 1.11). God is not taken by surprise at scientific discoveries. He is there behind it all, in His creatorial majesty.

"All things have been created by Him and **for** *Him"* (v. 7) The Apostle Paul raises a similar doxology: *"For of Him and through Him and unto Him are all things. To him be glory for ever"* (Rom.

11:36). God derives pleasure from His creation. Ultimately His own purpose and will is the reason behind all created things, and when the time is ripe He will *"fold it up as a garment"* (Heb. 1:12) and will create new heavens and a new earth.

With an economy of words, the Apostle John is inspired to write: *"Behold, I make all things new"* (Rev. 21:5). The new creation is described in negatives, rather than in positives. We will have to wait to see what the Creator has planned for the eternity to come.

Christ's Ones

"... your body is the temple of the Holy Ghost... you are not your own.... Therefore glorify God in your body, and in your spirit, which are God's" (Cor. 6:19-20).

All believers in the Lord Jesus are Christians—**Christ's ones**!

To be a Christian means to belong to Christ. In His death, He made a purchase that led to ownership. He now has two claims upon us: His **creatorial right**, and His **redemptive right.**

It was sovereign, electing grace that made us His own.

There are, however, serious implications arising out of this purchase! One of the main ones is that we should be *"zealous of good works."*

In the days of the Lord, a Zealot was an uncompromising partisan, or freedom fighter, of the extreme sect of the Pharisees. In Moslem speak, he would be pursuing a *jihad*—a holy war. He would have been vehemently opposed to the Roman authorities and, in a covert fashion, would have sought, with all means available to him, to harass and, if possible, destroy the government, the Roman occupying power.

In the same way Christians are in a Holy war against 'principalities, powers, the world, flesh and the devil' and we have to be zealous of—to ardently pursue, to prosecute—"**Good works!**" It is well to remember that we do this, not to procure our salvation, but because we already belong to the Lord Jesus.

Another implication of being a Christian is that all that we are and have are His!—body, soul and spirit. Therefore our actions must have the clear objective of bringing glory to the One who saved us, and now possesses us. We can do this in our worship as well as our witness.

What He has wrought inwardly—in causing us to praise His great and glorious Name will also manifest itself outwardly—in our behaviour to our fellow Christians and to the people that make up our world.

Constraining Love

"For the love of Christ constraineth us; because we thus judge that if one died for all, then were all dead: And that he died for all, that they which live should not henceforth live unto themselves but unto him who died for them and rose again" (2 Cor. 5:14-15).

Dr. Paul Rees, in his little book *If God Be For Us*, entitles this section, "Love Slaves of Jesus Christ." When we take the time to consider the Apostle's opening words, we get the feeling that this is no throw-away remark and certainly not the sentiments of a thoughtless soul. It is surely the language of intensity, coming from a heart bubbling over with devotion to his Lord.

When teaching the Word, I often draw attention to the possibility of taking one-word sermons from a text of Scripture. Here is a classic example:

*"The **love** of Christ constraineth us."*

*"The love of **Christ** constraineth us."*

*"The love of Christ **constraineth** us."*

*"The love of Christ constraineth **us.**"*

I don't know which of these four you think is the best. Each of them amazes me, and causes me to bow in holy worship. Perhaps today you will allow the pure word of God to pour into, through and out of your whole being, like rivers of living water (John 7:48.)

I.

*"The **love** of Christ constraineth us"*

The of the New Testament translates a number of Greek words, *Authorized Version*, as **love**. We now look briefly at two of these: *phileo* and *agapé*.

Phileo is a concept that demands equality of affection, as demonstrated by the love of one person for another. It has everything to do with warm reciprocation. Simon Peter used this word when replying to His Master's question: *"Simon, son of Jonas lovest* (agapé) *thou me?"* The answer came back three times: *"I have deep affection* (phileo) *for you"* He was saying that he loved on the only level he really knew how, and we must not think harshly of him for this.

He would have to learn that the **love** of Christ surpassed that level of love. This *agapé* **love** of Christ acts regardless of reciprocation. It sees nothing attractive in the one it loves, but it is a love that sees potential worth, value and esteem in worthless people— loving us when we were enemies and sinners (Rom. 5:6).

It saw value and worth in Saul of Tarsus though he was a blasphemer and persecutor of the saints! Hear his testimony, written years later: *"The Son of God loved me and gave himself for me"* (Gal. 2:20). That love led Christ to Golgotha to die for Saul of Tarsus—**and for us!**

The Apostle, writing to the church in Corinth, cannot restrain himself. He bursts out with all the passion he can muster: the **love of Christ constrains us**, and very definitely **included** himself!

> Love that no tongue can teach,
> Love that no thought can reach,
> No love like His!
> God is its blessed source,
> Death cannot stop its course,
> Nothing can stay its force,
> **Matchless it is!**
>
> —Thomas Kelly

II.

"The love of Christ constraineth us"

The Apostles love to use the expression: **Lord Jesus Christ.** It is important for us in our day and generation to ascribe

Him all honour, praise and worship to Him in the fullest way.

LORD: His TITLE

Scripture describes Him as:

The Lord out of heaven (1 Cor. 15:47).

Thee Lord of glory (1 Cor. 2:8).

The Lord of the living and the dead (Rom. 14:9).

Lord of all (Acts 10:38).

These are some references; you will recall others.

JESUS: His NAME

And what a Name it is!

"His Name shall be called Jesus, For he shall save his people from their sins" (Matt. 1:12).

Yeshua means **Saviour.**

Joseph was given the title Zaphenath –Paneah by Pharaoh – suggested by some to be the saviour of the land (Egypt). In their hunger the people were told to go to Joseph; he held the key to the storehouses of life and salvation.

And so the name remains the same down the centuries, the **only** Saviour for my hunger and the giver of eternal life.

CHRIST: His OFFICE

Christos— the Greek translation of the Hebrew Messiah, the Anointed of Jehovah.

Three kinds of people were anointed in Old Testament times; prophets, priests and kings. Our Lord Jesus Christ is the **only** One who bears all three offices!

Great are the offices He bears,
And bright His character appears,
Exalted on the throne,

In songs of sweet untiring praise,
We would through everlasting days,
Make **all His glories** known.

—Samuel Medley

The practical message for today is that He is Sovereign, Ruler, King of my whole being. This is the context of the nature of the love I am to show.

It is the love of **Christ**!

III.

*"The love of Christ **constraineth** us"*

That is, it impels, drives and motivates. Someone has defined the word **constrain** in a sentence: 'The love of Christ shuts me up to a single purpose as between two walls in a narrow path.'

Do you remember the story of Baalam?

He drove his donkey down a road in defiance of God and kept goading the beast forward until it was pressed between two walls. Unable to turn right or left, it sank down on its knees and refused to budge. And then it spoke to Baalam!

This is a perfect illustration of what it means to **constrain** or to be **constrained**. You can only move forward or not move at all.

The Apostle says, in effect, I have no option, when I think of the value and esteem my Lord placed on me—a blasphemer and persecutor. I have to return that love in the only way open to me. That is I must be an **ambassador** for Him, pleading with men to be reconciled to God (v. 20). And, if that preserves my life or takes me to death, *"for me to live is Christ and to die is gain"* (Phil. 1:2).

Too often we seem to reverse the order by how we live, 'For us to live is gain and die is Christ'! For the Christian the latter is true, but the former doesn't follow.

IV.

*"The love of Christ constraineth **us**."*

What can be said about the last of these one-word sermons?

There could possibly be some explanation to this, if the **us** represented a God fearing and obedient people. Sadly, the whole saga of human history is one of total failure and repeated disappointment to God. Time after time, because of his unfailing love, God gave mankind a fresh start. But more often than not, man made a mess of it.

We do not need to appeal only to scripture to prove this. We need to look no further than our own thoughts and actions. Apart from the regenerating power of God and the presence of the indwelling Holy Spirit, we will continue to fail miserably.

The Apostle, writing to the Ephesian Christians, puts the **us** in its proper and only context:

"And you hath he quickened who were dead in trespasses and sins. Wherein in time past, ye walked according to the course of this world, according to the prince of the power of the air, the spirit that now worketh in the children of disobedience. Among whom we also had our conversation (manner of life) *in times past in the lusts of our flesh, fulfilling the desires of the flesh and of the mind and were by nature the children of wrath, even as others. But God who is rich in mercy for his great love where with he loved us, even when we were dead in sins, hath quickened us together with Christ* (by grace ye are saved). *And hath raised us up together and made us sit together in heavenly places in Christ Jesus...."*

I am so glad that I am included in the **us**! Are you?

V.

"Therefore if any man be in Christ, he (there) is a new creation; old things have passed away, behold, the new has come" (2 Cor. 5:17).

In the regenerated life, there are two areas where love is dominant:

1. in our salvation—love is the **power** (vv. 14-19)
2. in our service—love gives us **passion** (vv. 20-25)

There has never been a day when the world needs more saving than today. There are more people lost, hopeless and in despair than ever before. Modern man, in his Godless self-centredness, is daily finding more ways of departure from his Creator. Somehow we seem to be failing to communicate to people that salvation is not found in religion, politics or reformation, but in Christ. It is time for a redoubling of our efforts to proclaim the gospel- the whole gospel and nothing but the gospel.

"...they which live should not henceforth live unto themselves but unto him which died for them and rose again" (v. 15).

Yes, Christians need saving too! Many are losing themselves in this world's business and pleasure. Scripture plainly warns us not to *"entangle ourselves with the affairs of this life"* (2 Tim. 2:4). The shelves of Christian bookstores are lined with auto-biographies and biographies of men and woman who found that love for Christ displaced all selfish ambition and power-drunkenness. Love for Him was the ruling motive of their lives, it was the power of daily salvation—and **ours**!

While at college, Jim Elliot, the martyr in Ecuador wrote:

> "O God, save me from a life of barrenness, follow-ing a formal pattern of ethics, and give instead that vital contact of soul with Thy divine life, that fruit may be produced, and life—abundant life—may be known again, as the final proof for Christ's mes-sage and work."

VI.

"Now then we are ambassadors for Christ, as though God did beseech you by us; we pray you in Christ's stead, be ye reconciled to God" (2 Cor. 5:20).

We now see that, for the Apostle Paul, the constraining love of Christ gave him a **passion** in his service. Think of the high honour bestowed on an individual: an **ambassador!** And an ambassador for **Christ**!

We know that an ambassador is invested with the authority of the Head of State of his country, to represent him, his government and country in a foreign state. We have been commissioned, authorized and sent out throughout the world to represent the King of heaven. He commands us to stand out and stand up for Him, to proclaim His worth, His glory, His Lordship and His kingdom—the kingdom of heaven to all mankind.

No one in heaven's diplomatic circles is more pleasing to the King than the name of the simplest believer who, in school, university, workplace or home, witnesses to Him.

However, it will not always be as it is now. The high King, in His longsuffering, is withholding wrath and awful vengeance from a rebellious world. Make no mistake, this must not be interpreted as non involvement! **It will end** and **soon**. Did not the Lord say, " *I must work the works of him that sent me while it is day, the night cometh when no man can work*" (John 9:4). This is love's protest against procrastination. It is love's denial of the right to drift on and fritter away our lives, while the time bomb of God's judgement ticks on.

So, it is not only an honour to be called to and involved in this service, but the Apostle senses the need for haste, as he urges us not to misuse the time:

For the ambassador *"now is the accepted time, now is the day of salvation"* (2 Cor. 6:2).

Discipleship

"If any man will come after me let him deny himself and take up his cross daily and follow me" (Luke 9:23).

Cross-bearing is not a once-for-all act, nor is it carrying the daily pressure of life that arises due to our humanity. The cross is not forced upon us against our will. Many who say they are disciples of Christ, show by their words and actions that they know nothing of this voluntary but deliberate daily task.

If it is not bearing the afflictions of life or a once-for-all act of dedication to the Lord; what is it?

The phrase *"take up his cross daily"* is bracketed between two companion phrases, *"let him deny himself"* and *"follow me"* These together give us an understanding of cross bearing. Self denial is not a natural ingredient of human nature. We all, to some degree or other, have an 'ego' in our lives. The capital 'I' or the pronoun 'me' are part of everyday speech.

The Apostle Paul, in his letter to the Philippian church, sets out his 'I' credentials. Seven of them, no less! But he quickly renounces these when he declares, *"Howbeit, those things that were gain to me, those I have counted loss for Christ"* (Phil. 3:5-7).

Jesus, in His dissertation to the disciples, uses the words *"must suffer...and be rejected"* (Matt. 16:31). Now the Apostle emulates His Master and exclaims *"....for whom I have suffered the loss of all things..."*. This is the death blow to priority thinking, beautifully and simply expressed in the children's chorus, "Jesus first, yourself last and **nothing** in between." The Apostle's only aim was to "win Christ" and this encompassed **all** life's experiences. There are no graduations of loyalty, no plan "B".

From the inception of the Church, cross bearing has been a repetitive occurrence. When Peter and John were released, after being beaten, *"they departed from the Council rejoicing that they were counted worthy to suffer dishonour for his name"* (Acts 5:41). We might ask, what is the reason for the suffering or the source of the dishonour? When the angel opened the prison doors, he commanded them to *"stand and speak in the temple the words of this Life"* (Acts 5:20). The Apostles were proclaiming the gospel of their crucified, risen and exalted Lord. For a perishing world the only source of true life is saving contact with the Life himself. Jesus said *"I am the way, the truth and the life"* (John 14:6). *"I am come that they might have life, and that they might have it more abundantly"* (John 10:10).

The preaching of the Gospel down the centuries since, in many places in or world has resulted in persecutions and in some cases even death. The testimonies of present day "cross bearers" are recorded in number. Two examples will suffice:

> "You want me to say that I have changed my religion because somebody pushed me into it, or for the sake of money or to get a job. But you are lying. You should know that I changed because I found the truth. I will kiss the rope that hangs me, but I will never deny my faith" —Tahir Iqbal, Pakistan.

> "I would rather have the whole world against me, but know that the Almighty God is with me, be called an apostate, but know that I have the approval of the God of glory" —Mehide Dibaj. Iran, from his defence at his trial for apostasy.

In this Western post-Christian era of beliefs, where truth is relative and standards no longer absolute, the genuine believer may soon suffer the consequences of cross bearing. Our Lord's clear declaration the *"no man cometh unto the Father but by Me"* (John 14:6) and the Apostles confirmation *"neither is there salvation in any other for there is none other name under heaven, given among men, whereby we must be saved"* (Acts 4:12) may soon be tested under the "Anti-Terrorism, Crime and Securities Act 2001," passed by the European Union. It may well be from our generation that some will be called to suffer this dishonour for the Name of the One who is our Lord and Master.

Entry To The Kingdom

"And Jesus went through the cities and villages, teaching and journeying towards Jerusalem. Then said one unto him, Lord, are there few that be saved? And he said unto them, Strive to enter in at the strait gate; for many I say unto you, will seek to enter in, and shall not be able" (Luke 13:22-24).

At this time the Lord Jesus is pressing on relentlessly to Jerusalem. The main purpose for his coming into the world was drawing closer. Despite the interventions and interruptions on the way, He does not allow Himself to be deviated from His purpose to save the lost, by giving His life a ransom.

In the course of events He was asked a curious question: **"Are there few that be saved?"**

The Lord appears to have ignored the question, but in reality He used it to spell out the issues of eternal life and death. He points out that people who are certain of being saved because they are sons of Abraham, would be outside the Kingdom and outside for ever. There was no guarantee that Israel's religious elite would be in the Kingdom either. They had their feet on the very threshold of the Kingdom of God, but were not disposed to enter on the conditions outlined by the young Rabbi from Galilee.

It reminds me of *Pilgrim's Progress*. As Christian approaches the Celestial City on his journey from the City of Destruction, he sees that near to its gates there is a way that leading down to the eternal abyss.

Why were these sons of Abraham in danger of exclusion? For the same reason that all mankind, of every age—ancient and modern—could be excluded. Many are trying to enter on the basis of their own righteousness! Try telling the self-righteous and the religious that they must repent of their sins and enter the Kingdom in the same way as a little child. The only way is to trust Jesus, the Messiah, as Saviour. Until this is acknowledged and acted upon, He cannot be their Lord.

In other words, entry into the Kingdom of God depends not on what we **are** or **do**, but on what He has **done**!

God's Harvest Field

I. THE PRAYER FOR LABOURERS

"When he saw the multitudes, he was moved with compassion on them, because they fainted, and were scattered abroad, as sheep having no shepherd. Then saith he unto his disciples, the harvest truly is plenteous, but the labourers are few; pray ye therefore the Lord of the harvest, that he will send labourers into his harvest" (Matt. 9:36-38).

All who look out on the national and international scene, whose hearts vibrate with love for lost souls, will empathize with the Lord in this compassionate expression of His inner soul. People all around are crying out in political, moral and spiritual distress. The latter may not recognize it as such, they just know they have a hunger and an emptiness which nothing they have tried has been able to satisfy.

We need to join our hands and hearts to fulfil the Lord's command. *"Pray ye therefore, the Lord of the harvest, that he will send forth labourers into his harvest."* Labourers to do what?

To reap a harvest of souls into the Kingdom of God!

Some have already been sent, some are in the process of being sent and there are those who will yet hear that call to leave all and follow Him. But equally important, there are those who will stay 'at home'. They can serve too, efficiently and effectively. They **must pray**!

Can the Lord of the harvest not gather in His harvest without our prayers? Yes, of course He can! **But** He wants us to be involved with Him in this great reaping and to be fulfilled in our relationship with Him. *"The sower and the reaper will then rejoice together"* (John 4:36).

II. THE PRINCIPLE OF LABOURING

"These twelve Jesus sent forth, and commanded them, saying, Go not into the way of the Gentiles, and into any city of the Samaritans

enter ye not: But go rather to the lost sheep of the house of Israel" (Matt. 10:5-6).

Why the prohibition in regard to the Gentiles and the Samaritans? Were they not lost, and part of the harvest? They were, perhaps even more lost, distressed and in need of the Shepherd's salvation. Could the finger of accusation be levelled at the Lord for discrimination, partiality or even apathy?

Why go just to Israel? He was not a racist nor was He partial. He was the **King** of Israel. But He was more, He was the true **Shepherd** of Israel (John 10:1). In saving Israel first, He would send them as ambassadors both to the Samaritans and to the whole Gentile world. The principle has been followed through as recorded by the Lord to His disciples *"... in Jerusalem, Judea, Samaria and the uttermost parts of the earth"* (Acts 1:8-9).

Here we are now, the harvested of God, enjoying the blessings of Eternal Life.

In truth, we owe our salvation to the Jews! (John 4:22).

The Samaritans need to be saved. This is why the Lord reached out, to the consternation of His disciples, and gave Living water, to the woman from Sychar!

And Philip, the evangelist went to the city of Samaria and *"preached Christ unto them, and the people with one accord gave heed unto those things which Philip spoke"* (Acts 8:5-6).

The Gentiles need to be saved also. That is why the Lord blessed the Syrophoenician woman (Mark 7:26), and why He sent Peter on a curious mission up the Mediterranean coast from Joppa to Caesarea to tell Cornelius, the Roman Centurion, that **Jesus is Lord of all** (Acts 10:1-36).

III. THE PLAN FOR LABOURING

"Behold." Pay special attention to this! The Master says to His disciples: "This is My plan, this is how I will gather the harvest." *"I send you forth as sheep in the midst of wolves."*

This is the "I" of deity! He is not only the Source of the

gospel, He is the Sustainer of the ministry and the Supplier of strength for the labourers.

Can you imagine a sheep surrounded by wolves! What possible chance of survival does it have?

It would be frightening enough to find oneself in such a situation by accident, but to be sent into it, is beyond belief! Perhaps, now, we can see the necessity of the Master's, *"Behold."*

The wonder of the plan does not stop there. Puzzling as it is, to see preachers of the Kingdom, defenceless as sheep, surrounded by hostility and persecution (and for some it would result in martyrdom), it is even more astonishing to anticipate the salvation of the wolves!

But this is God's plan, God's way of saving the world. He was going to save people not by fighting but by dying. And so it has ever been, the great Harvest—Maker is still sending for His sheep. But let us not be deceived. The world is no less hostile today than it was when Stephen was killed in the stoning pit for the cause of his rejected Master.

It just so happened that one of the "wolves" that surrounded the defenceless Stephen was Saul of Tarsus!

IV. THE PRESSURES OF LABOURING

"Beware of men: for they will deliver you up to the councils… and ye shall be brought before governors and kings for my sake… But when they deliver you up, take no thought how or what ye shall speak… for it is not ye that speak, but the Spirit of your Father which speaketh in you…And ye shall be hated of all men for my name's sake…it is enough for the disciple that he be as his master… Whosoever therefore shall confess me before men, him will I confess also before my Father which is in heaven" (Matt. 10:17-32).

Humanly speaking, this is a catalogue of disincentives to follow the Master! And all spelled out in such a matter-of-fact way. The disciples were made aware that service for Him would not be an easy option; preaching the gospel of the Kingdom of God would not make them popular.

In the Master's message there was certainly enough to cause them to have second thoughts. To return to their former employment may have brought short term benefits, but in the long term, it would have been disastrous, both for them **and** for us!

Short term expediency is not the way to judge the success of a mission. And, as if to emphasize this point, no sooner had the Messiah come, than John, the forerunner, was put into prison (Matt. 11:2). The long awaited Deliverer and Anointed of God seemed to be in difficulties too: they said He was a glutton and a drunkard and a friend of tax collectors and sinners (v.19). Not a lot of encouragement here for the disciples.

But the truth is that *"these things are hidden from the wise and prudent and revealed unto babes"* (Matt. 11:25).

V. PROMISE FOR THE LABOURER

"Come unto me all ye that labour and are heavy laden and I will give you rest. Take my yoke upon you and learn of me for I am meek and lowly in heart; and ye shall find rest unto your souls. For my yoke is easy and my burden is light" (Matt. 11:28-30).

What precious words for the disciples to hear. The Master was promising them **rest**.

That would come as they leant on Him and learned from Him. But it seems strange that to get rid of one heavy load you have to take on another one!

"Take my yoke." This is a voluntary action. It is not imposed on unwilling shoulders. Each disciple must be ready and willing to take it on. The key to the apparent contradiction is, of course, that the Master Himself would be the other partner in the yoke! It was designed for two evenly selected load carriers. Scripture tells us that God hates unequal yokes (2 Cor. 6:14). The yoke they and we enter with Him will be balanced and equally distributed on both shoulders. It must not be too heavy because that would prevent any work from being done. Nor must it be too light for that, too, would hinder the proper execution of the task.

So the Master is saying to the disciples and to all potential Kingdom preachers, "When you bear the trial, the pain, the humiliation, I am with you, beside you in the yoke, on an equal level."

That surely is sufficient to remove all doubts and fears.

But even better, He promises they will *"find rest* (a different word from v. 28) *for their souls"*, that is, for their inner lives. In modern days terms, they would have job satisfaction. Their minds would be unstressed and they would be able to rest as they worked.

In my working life I have found that a good day's satisfactory work was more restful than lying for hours on a beach!!

As the saying goes, 'THE PROOF OF THE PUDDING IS IN THE EATING.'

God's Pleasure In His Son

"This is my beloved son, in whom I am well pleased; hear ye him" (Matt. 17:5; 2 Pet. 1:17).

"Yet it pleased the Lord to bruise him, he hath put him to grief, when Thou shalt make his soul an offering for sin, he shall see his seed, he shall prolong his days and the pleasure of the Lord shall prosper in his hand" (Isa. 53:10).

The Father's pronouncement of His pleasure in His Son is a demonstration of unspeakable glory, *"His face shone as the sun... and His raiment was white and glistering"* It caused the watching disciples to fall on their faces. It was not that humans should fall before such glory, it was God , the Father, taking pleasure in the radiance of His Son. He reveals Him in blinding light and says "This is My pleasure."

In measure, as humans, we can understand this revealing of God in His Son, in a scene of resplendent glory. What we find quite beyond us is an explanation of the prophet Isaiah's word, *"Yet it pleased the Lord to bruise Him"*! Where do we start in an attempt to interpret the Lord's heart? In his book *The Pleasures Of God*, John Piper refers to the "Great tension of the ages. The harmonising of two opposites: On the one hand God's passion to promote His pleasure and His glory and on the other, God's electing love for sinners that scorned that glory."

The answer to the great question of how sinful humanity can be reconciled to a holy and righteous God was given seven hundred years before the birth of Christ. It was by the bruising and putting to death of His Son. And the staggering thing is that God took pleasure in it! He was not slain by man in an uncontrollable frenzy. He was, as the Apostle Peter states, *"delivered by the determinate counsel and foreknowledge of God"* (Acts 2:23).

We might ask, Why did God do this? He did it to accomplish the task that would bring Him the **ultimate pleasure**!—that we, sinners of a fallen race, might be reconciled to Him! This is the ultimate glory spoken of by the Apostle John in his Gospel chapter 17:24, *"Father, I will that them whom Thou hast given Me,* *be with Me where I am that they may behold My glory."* Why could our sin not be ignored and a merciful God overlook it? Because God loves the honour of His Name. He cannot act as though sin, which belittles His glory, doesn't matter. So heinous in the sight of God is man's sin and human guilt that it demanded the death of God Incarnate. What an awesome thought! In Proverbs 17:15, we read, *"He who justifies the wicked is an abomination to the Lord."* In our day, we are enraged when guilty men go free, yet at the heart of the Christian Gospel is the doctrine that God justifies the ungodly and acquits the guilty! But how can He do that and remain righteous? Again, He Himself gives us the answer through His apostle, *"...justified, freely, by His grace through the redemption that is in Christ Jesus"* (Rom. 3:24). Everything the Lord Jesus suffered He suffered for God's pleasure and glory. He cannot and will not under any circumstances fail God. He speaks with authority, *"I do always those things that please Him* [the Father]*"* (John 8:29). He also said, referring to His death, *"Now is the Son of man glorified and God is glorified in Him"* (John 13:31). All the pain, the shame, the humiliation, the dishonour, would bring glory to His Father. He was determined that through suffering and death, Satan and all hosts that had brought unimaginable pain and death into His creation, would be defeated, and ensure that God's righteous character would not be tarnished. God would justify sinners and retain His glory because He Himself (in the person of His Son) became answerable for our iniquity. This is the Gospel—God's good news! And Ephesians 5:2 tells us that the sacrifice of Christ was *"an odour of a sweet smell"*—a fragrant aroma to God.

Our text goes on to say: *"He shall see His seed and the pleasure of the Lord shall prosper in His hand."* Here was an additional way that God would derive pleasure, that despite being *"cut off out of the land of the living,"* unmarried and without offspring, he would *"see the travail of his soul and be satisfied"* in other words, as Hebrews 2:10 puts it, *"For it became Him, for whom are all things, and through whom are all things, in bringing many sons unto glory, to make the captain* [pioneer] *of their salvation perfect through suffering."* And again in verse 13 *"...behold I and the children which God hath given me."*

The Pioneer:

He tackles the seemingly impossible.

He does what no one has done before.

He triumphs over every difficult circumstance.

And now finally, we need to ask, Is this justification automatic? We return again to Romans 3:22: *"...through faith in Jesus Christ unto all them that believe."* The Apostle goes on to say that there is no distinction between Jew and Gentile, *"for all have sinned and come short* [missed the mark] *of the glory of God."* There we have it again, *"the **glory of God**."* This is the beginning and end of the matter. It is this that we are declaring when we preach the Gospel. In its proclamation let us carefully and prayerfully interpret the Word remembering that God's honour and glory is at stake.

Grace Demonstrated

MATTHEW 20:1-16

This is an exceptional story; in terms of logic and fairness it is unsurpassed. It begins with a householder, or employer, hiring workers to work in his vineyard on a daily basis. He commences early in the morning, finds those who want work and agrees to a daily wage. Three hours later he decides to hire more, and again at the sixth and ninth hours, by agreement, he takes on more workers.

We are surprised to find that he decides to employ some at the eleventh hour who have been unable to find employment. *"You go also into the vineyard,"* he commands. Those who started in the morning had a long tiring day in contrast to those who worked for only one hour.

Now the time has arrived for the payment of the wages. In my mind's eye I see them standing in line. He instructs the foreman to pay out the money beginning with those whom he had employed for the last hour. He pays them one *denarius* (translated, a penny). Those who worked for the whole day, when they saw this, expected to be paid more. But they too received just a penny. Naturally they were very upset and complained, *"These last have spent but one hour, and you have made them equal unto us, which have borne the burden of the day and the scorching heat."* In today's language, they were protesting that it wasn't fair!

However the employer replied to the protesting spokesman *"Friend I do you no wrong, did you not agree with me for a penny? Take that which is yours and go your way; it is my will to give unto this last what I have given to you! Is it not lawful for me to do what I will with my own money?"* We have to accept on the basis of the contract that was made with each of the workers that they had no grounds for complaint, despite the apparent unfairness.

But look at it from the employer's standpoint, What employer, in his right mind, would pay the same for one hour's work as for twelve? It makes no economic sense. What then is

34

the point Jesus was making when he said this was 'the kingdom of Heaven'?

This is a marvellous illustration of **grace**! Grace is not based on economics! Simply put, grace is giving what is not deserved. Grace cannot be calculated like a day's wages. The Scriptures tell us: *"That by grace we are saved through faith; and that not of yourselves, it is the **gift of God"** (Eph. 2:8).

The last little phrase of the employer to the workers in verse 15 is important. To paraphrase it he said, "Are you envious because I am generous?" We like to think of ourselves as responsible workers. We sympathize with the complaint of those who had toiled all day. But if we do , we miss the point; God dispenses gifts **not** wages! In the kingdom of God, none of us gets paid according to merit, for none of us comes close to God's requirement of righteousness. If paid on the basis of fairness we would all end up in hell!

It was C.S. Lewis who remarked, "To be a Christian means to forgive the inexcusable, because God has forgiven the inexcusable in us." We live in a society which expects people to get what they deserve. But the Gospel of grace says, "you have by faith got what you don't deserve." The Apostle Paul called himself, *"the chief of sinners."* See him on his way to Damascus, *"breathing threatening and slaughter against the disciples of the Lord"* with letters in his pocket from the high priest, *"...that if found any of the Way that he might bring them bound unto Jerusalem"* (Acts 9:1-2). Previously he had stood with the clothes of the murderers of Stephen at his feet, as guilty as they were. He now lies blinded and prostrate on the road, struck down by the very One he was persecuting. What do you think he deserved? Fairness cries out; punish him! Grace responds, *"...he is a chosen vessel unto Me!"* (Acts 9:16). Until his dying day he never recovered from or fully understood the impact of grace! Over and over again in his letters he pours out his heartfelt thoughts as he tries to get a grip on what John Newton called **amazing grace**. Let us listen to him: *"For scarcely for a righteous man will one die: for peradventure for the good man some would even dare to die. But God commendeth his own love towards* *us that while we were yet sinners, Christ died for us. Much more then, being now justified by his blood, we shall be saved from wrath through him. For if when we were enemies we were reconciled to God, much more we shall be saved by His life. And not only so, but we also rejoice in God, through our Lord Jesus Christ, through whom we have now received the reconciliation"* (Rom. 5:7-11). And again, *"This is a faithful saying, worthy of all acceptation, that Christ Jesus came into the world to save sinners; of whom I am chief* [foremost]*"* (1 Tim. 1:15). The reason, I believe, the Apostle never got over the truth of God's grace is because in the above statement he continues to use the present tense! *"I **am** chief."*

In concluding we take up the words of Julia H. Johnston:

Marvellous grace of our loving Lord,
Grace that exceeds our sin and our guilt
Yonder on Calvary's mount outpoured,
There's where the blood of the Lamb was spilt.

Marvellous, infinite, matchless grace,
Freely bestowed on all who believe,
You, who are longing to see His face,
Will you this moment His grace receive?

Humanity Glorified

In John chapter seventeen there are seven requests from the Son to the Father. The first one, may seem strange to us at first glance. It had to do with His humanity being glorified. Listen to His prayer:

"I have glorified thee on the earth: I have finished the work which thou gavest me to do. And now, O Father,glorify thou me with thine own self with the glory which I had with thee before the world was" (John 17:4-5).

As the eternal Son, one would think that His glory was beyond doubt. Why did He ask the Father for it?

A closer look reveals that He is referring to the glorification of His human nature which He acquired on earth, the body which had been prepared for Him and in which He lived. He is asking that it be received up and into the place of glory where He had always been. He described this to Nicodemus, *"He that came down from heaven, even the Son of Man who is in heaven"* (John 3:13). He is really praying that His manhood attain a status far beyond what normal humanity can reach.

Was the prayer answered?

Forty days after His resurrection His disciples witnessed His bodily ascension. Let us hear and ponder the words of the angel: *"This same Jesus which is taken up from you into heaven, shall so come in like manner* [that is in a literal body] *as ye have seen him go into heaven"* (Acts 1:12).

What did Stephen see as he was being stoned to death? *"He, being full of the Holy Ghost, looked steadfastly into heaven, and saw the glory of God, and **Jesus, standing on the right hand of God**"* (Acts 7:55). Luke also records that Jesus spoke to Saul of Tarsus on the Damascus road. Stephen and Paul were not hallucinating! They **saw** and we **believe**!

His humanity **was** glorified. The prayer was answered.

And—there is a man in the glory!

"Father I will that them thou hast given Me may be with Me where I am that they may behold My glory " (v. 24).

In this last request, He now asks the same for His disciples and all who would believe on Him—sons of a fallen Adamic race. He asks that they should be glorified with Him. This surely stretches the boundaries of human understanding.

Yet this is what He wants. It is His final request. To see this accomplished will be the zenith of His work.

As part of the prayer, he adds, *"You have loved me from before the foundation of the world"* What a plea to the Majesty on high! This must mean that the redemption and reconciliation of the Cross will be reflected in uncountable myriads of changed human beings—changed into the image of God's Son.

The hymn writer aptly put it:

> And is it so we shall be like Thy son,
> Is this the grace which He for us has won?
> Father of glory!, (thought beyond all thought),
> In glory to Thine own blest likeness brought.

The Apostle Paul, in his dissertation on the resurrection says, *"…As we have borne the image of the earthly, we shall also bear the image of the heavenly"*—and, as if to emphasize the enormity of the transformation, he adds *"…flesh and blood cannot inherit the kingdom of God, neither doth corruption inherit corruption. Behold, I shew you a mystery, we shall not all sleep but we* [believers] *shall all be changed. For this corruptible must put on incorruption and this mortal put on immortality"* (1 Cor. 15:49-51,53).

> Not we alone, Thy loved ones all complete,
> In glory, round Thee there with joy shall meet;
> All like Thee, for Thy glory like Thee Lord,
> Object supreme of all, by all adored.

HEART WARMING TRUTHS

The heart is satisfied, can ask no more,
All thought of self is now for ever o'er,
Christ, its unmingled object, fills the heart,
In blest adoring love the endless part.

—J. N. Darby

Imputed Righteousness

"And now apart from the law a righteousness of God has been manifested…" (Rom. 3:21).

"Abraham believed God and it was reckoned to him for righteousness …to him that worketh the reward is not reckoned of grace but as of debt. But to him that worketh not but believeth on him that justifieth the ungodly, his faith is reckoned for righteousness" (Rom. 4:3-5).

Nine times in this chapter the word *"reckoned"* is used and that is very significant as we shall see.

God reckons, pronounces or treats as righteous the ungodly who has **no** righteousness of his own to show.

It is his **faith** that is reckoned for righteousness. Faith in Christ is accepted instead of personal merit gained by good works.

This faith has Christ as its object (ch. 3:22), especially **propitiation** (the mercy seat) in His blood (ch. 3:25).

What is the result of this **faith** linked to **reckoning**? That is

Faith on the part of the sinner.

Reckoning on the part of God.

It is important to note that the Apostle does not speak anywhere of God transferring Christ's righteousness or merits to us as if they belonged to us. Such an actual transfer would demand that we become sinless. If this were so there would be no need of the **grace** spoken of in verse 4, and this surely is an obvious and present necessity in the life of the believer.

We conclude therefore that God does not impute (give) righteousness to the unrighteous but only through the process of sanctification based on the initial act of belief followed by justification can a person be released from the burden of guilt. Only then can he, by the indwelling Holy Spirit, begin to understand that he is truly forgiven and therefore should not and indeed cannot abuse the grace of God by continuing to sin (Romans chapter 6). Sanctification and justification go hand in hand.

To the apostle Paul this was an ongoing experience, beginning with his crucifixion with Christ at Golgotha... *"...I have been crucified with Christ..."* (Gal. 2:20). But the indwelling spirit would be ever present in the transforming of his character until the completion of redemption (Rom. 8:23). He found in His Lord and Master not only the gifts of justification and forgiveness, but also power to be holy! The amazing thing about all this is that He has done it all "without a cause." Excepting that it is His **love** that is at the heart of all that He **is**!

Incarnation

"Then Simeon took Him up in his arms and blessed God, and said, 'Lord, now lettest thou thy servant depart in peace, according to thy word: For mine eyes have seen Thy salvation which Thou hast prepared before the face of all people; a light to lighten the Gentiles, and the glory of Thy people Israel.' And Joseph and His mother marvelled at those things which were spoken of Him" (Luke 2:28-33).

So the Word became flesh and pitched his tent – His humanity—among us. Try to understand it, if you will. Meditate until you are lost in holy wonder.

The Ancient of Days, conceived in the womb of a virgin, held in the arms of His own creation, breathing His own air and supported by the substances that He himself had brought into being. He walked amid nature's elements, felt the wind in His face and the sharp dew of the morning as he arose from a night of prayer.

But the most amazing thing is that He, the Author of life, entered a scene of disease and death but remained untainted, untarnished, unspotted, flawless and faultless. Every syllable, word or sentence that the greatest scholar can find to describe His perfection, when it is all spoken, has not, in the smallest degree, told out His uniqueness.

Demon-filled swine rushed headlong to a watery grave in the Galilee. At the voice of the Son of God, blind see, lame walk and the dead rise. The Creator of the ends of the earth in His own world, but alas, unrecognized!

He wedded Himself to our flesh, partook of our humanity, never to go out of it any more. Unresistingly he went to Gethsemane, Gabbatha and Golgotha. There He poured out His soul unto death. The rocks split open, the sun refused to shine, the great veil of the temple was torn in the middle from top to bottom.

Nothing like it has happened before or since.

Now the light would shine to Gentiles, and the glory of God now and in the future to Israel.

Jesus Is Lord

"I give you to understand that no man speaking in the Spirit of God, saith Jesus is anathema (accursed); *and no man can say Jesus is Lord, but in the Holy Spirit"* (1 Cor. 12:3 - R.V.).

This is the test of true belief. *Anathema,* that which is devoted to God for destruction under His curse, was to say that instead of Christ being the Son of God as He claimed, He was an impostor and a blasphemer, bringing down God's judgement upon His head! This is why those who followed Jesus to the cross cried, *"His blood be on us* [our heads] *and on our children"* (Matt. 27:25). This referred back to Deuteronomy 19:10, *"that innocent blood be not shed in the midst of Thy land… and so blood be upon Thee."*

Thus the battle lines of opposing spiritual forces were drawn. Either He was *anathema* or **Lord**! And the apostle's message to these newly converted Corinthians was clear, only those indwelt by the Holy Spirit could rightly claim Him as their Lord. What therefore does it mean to be Lord? It is to believe that Jesus is God! Truly Man and truly God. We must be clear on this fundamental doctrine of apostolic teaching. The apostle Peter sets the stage in his address to the *"men of Israel"* and concludes with the declaration, *"let all the house of Israel know assuredly that God hath made Him both Lord* (title) *and Christ* (office), *this Jesus* (name) *whom ye crucified."* Much later on, this is confirmed by the apostle Paul (7:10); *"to us there is one God, the Father, of whom are all things and one Lord, Jesus Christ, through whom are all things"* (1 Cor. 8:6). In our lead text the apostle is really saying "You may say the words, make profession, but unless you are born of God you are false." It is blasphemous for professing Christians to deny the divinity and impeccability of Jesus. The acknowledgement of Jesus as Lord marks the beginning of *"new life"* for the believer and says *"**He is God**."* Isaiah sums it up in his declaration of God's greatness, *"Look unto Me and be ye saved all ye ends of the earth for I am God and there is none else"* (Isa. 45:22).

We need, in understanding the New Birth, to realize that we do not first trust Jesus as Saviour and then live to make Him

Lord! We cannot make Jesus Lord—He **is** Lord! Scripture clearly teaches that calling Jesus Lord is the language of salvation; *"If thou shalt confess with thy mouth Jesus as Lord and believe in thy heart, that God raised Him from the dead thou shalt be saved"* (Rom. 10:9), *"For whosoever, shall call upon the name of the Lord shall be saved"* (10:13). In other words, when we confess and believe in Him as Lord, He saves us. It is interesting to note that the confession relates to the resurrection and not to the cross and His death on our account. The resurrected and glorified Jesus was the proof of his promise; *"because I live ye shall live also"* (John 14:19). The cross was the victory, the resurrection the triumph!

What then does it mean to accept Jesus as Lord?

First, it is a matter of **ownership**. 1 Corinthians 6:19-20: *"What? know ye not that your body is the temple of the Holy Ghost which is in you, which ye have of God, and ye are not your own? For ye are bought with a price: therefore glorify God in your body, and in your spirit, which are God's."* The temple was the dwelling place of God characterized by holiness and reverence. The owner therefore was not man but God and we must use it only for the purpose for which it was designed—to glorify Him. Recognising this will help us to differentiate between truth and falsehood and to uphold integrity and morality in our testimony in the world.

In addition to the ownership of the individual believer there is the corporate aspect relating to the Church, His ecclesia! *"And he is the head of the body the church... that in all things he must have the pre-eminence"* (Col. 1:18). *"Christ loved the church and gave himself for it"* (Eph. 5:25). The visible expression of this is seen in each local gathering acknowledging His headship.

Second, **mastery** over his possession follows. The apostle Peter referring to false teachers says; *"denying even the Master that bought them"* (2 Pet. 2:1). The word used for master is "despot", meaning autocratic control. In the Biblical sense it does not carry the modern meaning of tyranny, rather that of a willing servants. *"Not as men-pleasers but as servants of Christ, doing the will of God from the heart"* (Eph. 6:6). This results, not only in individual fellowship with God, but in corporate worship.

It leads to **unity**. *"Giving diligence to keep the unity of the spirit in the bond of peace"* (Eph. 4:3). As we meet each Lord's day in remembrance of Him, as he commanded, He is in the midst. It is a sad betrayal of unity and a mockery of fellowship if there is disharmony among those who profess to call Him Lord, especially if it concerns those who are in leadership. Our meeting together in such a state is not only a waste of time but those responsible will be judged in a day to come. Church elders need to heed the teaching of the apostle Peter, not as doctrinal theory, but in heart and practice. *"The elders among you I exhort...Tend the flock of God which is among you.... not lording it over the charge allotted to you, but making yourselves examples to the flock"* (1 Pet. 5:1-11).

Third, **liberty**. *"Now the Lord is the Spirit; and where the Spirit of the Lord is there is liberty"* (2 Cor. 3:17). If the condition of our hearts individually or corporately is as described above, then fellowship will not be realized and the sense of the Lord's presence will be absent. But what a difference when ownership and mastery are truly acknowledged and with joy we meet to sing His praise, pour out our hearts in adoring worship, feed on the Bread of Life and agree with the Psalmist in 133. *"Behold how good and how pleasant it is for brethren to dwell together in unity! It is like the precious oil upon the head, that ran down upon the beard, even Aaron's beard; and came down upon the skirt of his garments; Like the dew of Hermon, that cometh down upon the mountains of Zion: for there the Lord commanded the blessing, even life for evermore."*

On the high priests breast were the twelve precious stones that represented all the tribes of Israel. As the anointing oil ran down from the head it saturated the beard which swept over all the stones! What a precious picture! No wonder the Lord as Lord will for us too **command the blessing**!

Jesus The Rabbi

Who was Jesus to the people of his generation? He was a Jew. He was clearly recognized as such by the Samaritan woman, *"How is it that thou being Jew askest drink of me which am a woman of Samaria?"* (John 4:9).

History records for us some of the main traits of the Jewish character; intensely offensive and fanatical, regarding themselves as holy, special favourites of God and extremely defensive of the traditions of the fathers. Self righteous, proud, arrogant, hypocritical, and despisers of outsiders.

How does it happen then that there is nothing of this Jew in Jesus? How could this model man, the perfect pattern of all ages grow, develop and mature over thirty years in Nazareth, when concerning it Nathaniel said; *"Can any good thing come out of Nazareth?"* (John 1:46). We could further ask the questions, who taught Him the principles He announced with such authority in His *"sermon on the mount"* (Matt. 5-7), or who was the role model who instilled into Him kindness, gentleness, compassion and love? Yet when and where it was necessary He spoke with authority silencing his critics with scathing words of intense rebuke. No one ever got the better of Him, despite the fact that time after time His critics tried to catch Him in His words and to thus humiliate Him. Always they were left to ponder the mystery of who He really was.

As to his speech, the soldiers sent to arrest Him, had to admit, *"Never man spake like this Man"* (John 7:40). The disciples who followed Him failed to comprehend Him and were led to exclaim in utter astonishment, *"What manner of man is this that even the winds and the sea obey Him?"* (Matt. 8:27). The special accolade given to Him came when He stood disrobed and bloodied in the presence of the Roman governor and the disreputable leaders of the nation, *"I bring Him forth to you* [said Pilate] *that you may know that I find no fault in Him"* (John 8:38, 19:4, 6). Note, three times over he said it. Some time previously, Jesus had challenged the religious elite with the stinging question; *"Which of you convinces Me of sin?"* (John 8:46). His enemies had said He was an impostor, *"We know that this Man is a sinner"* (John 8:24), and a blasphemer (Matt. 9:3). They now get their answer and from the lips of a heathen ruler!

But that is not all. As He was being nailed to the cross in the midst of intense agony He kept on repeating, *"Father forgive them for they know not what they do"* (Luke 23:34).

No ordinary mortal lived as He lived or died as He died! And of course death was not the end. Though His accusers and crucifiers never saw Him again, He completed the mission His Father had sent him to do when He was gloriously resurrected and ascended to where He came from—*"the right hand of the majesty on high"* (Heb. 1:3).

But the story of the Man, Christ Jesus is not finished. The words of the angels at His ascension are unambiguous; *"this same Jesus which is taken up from you into heaven shall so come in like manner as ye have seen Him go"* (Acts 1:8).

It is astonishing to think that our worship of this One is heightened by a heathen Governor when undoubtedly con-fused he cried; *"**Behold the Man!**"*

Veiled in flesh the Godhead see,
Hail incarnate Deity.

—Charles Wesley

Living Water

THE ROUTE THAT HE TOOK

"He [Jesus] *left Judea and departed into Galilee. And he must needs pass through Samaria"* (John 4:3-4).

This was a Divine 'needs be'. It was not a geographical necessity but a moral one. Reverently speaking, the Lord had no other choice. It was the constraint of sovereign grace. The performing of God's eternal decree demanded it. It was His will that the Samaritans should hear the good news about the Kingdom and that they would hear it from the lips of His beloved Son. There were chosen souls that He must bring to the Father. We remember the Lord's words, *"Other sheep I have which are not of this* [Jewish] *fold; them also I must bring"* (John 10 :16). We shall never appreciate the Gospel, or pray correctly for its progress, unless we understand that God is the first cause in salvation.

THE PLACE WHERE HE RESTED

"He cometh…near to the parcel of ground that Jacob gave to his son Joseph. Now Jacob's well was there, Jesus therefore being wearied with His journey, sat thus on the well" (vv. 5-6).

What a journey it was, not just the physical day-to-day walking north and south in the land, but the journey from the manger to the cross! This was a significant place for Him to rest. In his New Translation, J.N. Darby points out that the Egyptian name, *Zaphnath-paaneah* given by Pharaoh to Joseph, could be translated "sustainer of life" and "saviour of the world." All that remained of Joseph's body was a few bones, his saving work long since past. But now Jesus, God's Son, **Saviour of the world**, journeys to that place where, for all eternity, sin would be dealt with and humanity offered, in grace, salvation full and free.

THE QUESTION HE ASKED

"There cometh a woman of Samaria to draw water: Jesus saith under her, give me to drink" (v. 7).

This was no accidental meeting, God's hour had struck when she was to meet her Saviour. The Lord was at the well first. When it comes to salvation He is always first! I am reminded of the famous text, *"All that the Father giveth me shall come to me and him that cometh to me I shall in no wise cast out"* (John 6:37) The question we need to ask is, was He physically thirsty? It would seem from verse 34 that He was not physically hungry and by the same token, both food and drink to him were spiritual. He was thirsting to give this woman *"living water."* In His foreknowledge He knew there were many Samaritans to be saved. And the refreshment he had in mind was to minister His grace to needy sinners. She would have to receive before she should give.

THE DISCUSSION THAT FOLLOWED

In the subsequent discourse the Lord is weaning her away from the physical to the spiritual. He tells her about *"living water."* He excites her by saying that she would never thirst again, *"Give me this water that I thirst not, neither come hither to draw,"* she said. How is He going to get her mind off the physical and on to the spiritual? He does it through Deity! For this One, sitting on this well, is more than man. He is God in flesh. He knew her past life intimately; He knew she had had five husbands, (most unlikely they were all dead). He knew, presently, that she was living in adultery! But He also knew that she was thirsty to fill and satisfy her parched and hollow life. So He put his finger of Deity on her conscience and asks her to call her husband! The question, like an arrow, stabs her to the heart. So she, perceiving Him to be a prophet answers truthfully, *"I have no husband"* (v. 17). It is a solemn thought to be constantly overseen by Omniscience. The all-seeing, all-knowing God knows us intimately — *"our down sittings and our uprisings…"* (Ps. 139).

At this point, faced with the searching eyes of the Prophet, she seeks to recover lost ground by changing the subject! A common ploy used at times by us all! She launches out on a new but controversial subject: **worship** (v. 20).

Any topic that will deflect the convicting of sin, will be used, so she settles for an argument on the "place" of worship. Perhaps we should pause here and reflect on our attitude to worship. The Lord was concerned about getting her to the **Person** to be worshipped more than the **place**. The presence of Christ on earth was changing the method and manner of worship. It would no longer be in the Tabernacle, the Temple or Mount Gerizim but around the glorious person of our beloved Lord Jesus Christ. A new order of things was about to be established. Not now the Old Covenant—**Jehovah**, but the New Covenant—the **Father**. It is no longer that Gerizim is the wrong place and Jerusalem the right place, it will be where the Father and the Son are. It will be *"Where the two or three are gathered together in My name"* (Matt. 18:20).

To worship Him spiritually is to give God the homage of an instructed and enlightened mind and an affectionate heart. To worship truly, is to worship the Lord according to the truth—that is the revelation in His word that He has given of Himself.

What was the conclusion of the discussion? *"Come"* she said *"see a man that told be all things what ever I did. Is not this the Christ [Messiah]?"* (v. 29). What a lovely sequel, the physical superceded by the spiritual! Once there is a clear perception of Christ in the soul, once He is the centre of our thinking, the natural and fleshly loses its value. The love of Christ constrained her! For her to live was Messiah!

THE REBUKE HE ADMINISTERED

"Say not ye, there are yet four months, and then cometh harvest? behold, I say unto you, Lift up your eyes and look on the fields, for they are white already unto harvest" (v. 35).

Now, instead of being faint and weary the Lord is full of vigour and energy Even though He had eaten no natural food. His *"meat was to do the will of Him that sent Me and to finish His work"* (v. 34). The disciples, on the other hand, also, could not see past the physical. Now it was their turn to be taught a lesson on spiritual food; reaping a harvest for God. He is saying to them, Open your eyes, can you not see what I see? Samaritans who need *"living water"*! To the disciples Samaria was a most unlikely place to work in and harvest for their Master. As far as they were concerned there was a cultural problem with the Samaritans. They were "half-caste." It was not appropriate **yet** to bring them the good news of the kingdom. I believe their Master was frustrated, perhaps even angry, as He saw their lack of spiritual perception. He might have said to them, I have just ploughed a field, sowed a seed and reaped a harvest, sitting on a well. The Samaritans, He might have continued, are not only ripe, but over ripe for a spiritual harvest. "The fields which He observed, were not worldwide fields (although we so often interpret them as such). They were Samaritan fields, not across the seas, but just down the road, between the hills of Judea and the plains of Galilee. What a stinging rebuke. The conclusion of His assessment is clear, a mission, not of a week or a month but just two days. *"And many more believed on Him, because of His words"* (v. 41).

In the Lord's work of propagating the Gospel, I have come to believe that if the conditions are right, fields that at first appear difficult turn out be not as difficult as they appeared.

Loosing The Moorings

"For I am now ready to be offered, and the time of my departure is at hand, I have fought a good fight, I have finished my course, I have kept the faith: Henceforth there is laid up for me a crown of righteousness, which the Lord, the righteous judge will give to me at that day: and not to me only, but unto all them also that love His appearing" (2 Tim. 4.6-8).

The Apostle sees his sacrifice as a drink offering poured out—offered on the altar of love to the Lord whom he served as a bond slave. Free and yet not free, because now, his life is about to climax in a death full of surrender to the will of God. *"The time of My departure is at hand."*

The Lord's servant was immortal until his work was finished, or Nero could not have ended his life. The word "departure" has been defined as follows: The separation—or the detaching—of one thing from another.

The untying of a cord,

Taking up the tent pegs,

Loosing the moorings.

The Apostle would soon weigh anchor and slip out of this earthly harbour to the "haven of rest" on the Celestial shore.

This is not to under estimate the awfulness of death. Scripture describes it as *"the last enemy"* (1 Cor. 15.28). But for the believer there is something about death that is solid, sure and safe, for our Anchor is within the veil—our Forerunner, even Jesus, is already there!

As well as looking forward, the Apostle reminisces about the past and we hear him say: *"I have fought a good fight."*

He casts a swift but searching glance over his life, and sums it up in three sentences, using the figures of a wrestler, a runner and a soldier. For it, he trained hard. The wrestler's arena is now empty, the cinder track is behind him, and the agony of warfare is finally over. He then adds: *"I have kept the faith."*

He has safely guarded the deposit of truth which was entrusted to him through revelation. He has been loyal to the truth of the gospel. His defence of it has been exemplary. He leaves for heaven and home with no regrets!

What an example to follow!

Moral Excellence

"Thou sayest that I am a king. To this end was I born, that I should bear witness to the truth" (John 18:37).

"And if I say the truth why will ye not believe me" (John 8:46).

Frankness, plain open speaking and truthfulness rank high when we consider the moral excellence of our Lord Jesus Christ. As He walked amongst people He had no pretence. His candour and truthfulness were an integral part of His everyday walk.

Even in the best of people, politeness and expediency take the edge off truthfulness. In all walks of life being economical with the truth is commonplace. Not so with the Lord Jesus. He was unmercifully candid. He was never rude or crude, but He never varnished his language to please His hearers.

The startling expression in Matthew 21:31, when confronted by the chief priests and elders, bears witness to this. *"The publicans* [tax collectors] *and harlots go into the kingdom of God before you."* They believed; you did not! He was not prepared to say in their absence what He could not say in their presence. On another occasion he accused the same people, *"This people honours me with their lips , but their hearts are far from me"*(Matt. 15:8).

Think, too, of the late night discussion with Nicodemus. The eminence of the visitor did not deter Him from pronouncing words that shocked the good man to the point of enquiring, *"How can these things be"* (John 3.9). He had already said, *"Except a man be born again he cannot see the kingdom of God"* (John 3:3). There was no diplomatic softening of the message. He would meet the man's enquiring mind with the truth. Ecclesiastical merit was insufficient. There could be no special exemption for a member of the Sanhedrin. He must enter the kingdom of God, by the new birth, like everyone else.

This is moral excellence.

The Lord's dealing with the Samaritans, too, astonished among the disciples and infuriated the Pharisees. He broke all convention by speaking to the Samaritan woman. (John 4:29).

But it led to her believing on Him! In Luke 17:16 a Samaritan returned to thank Him for his cleansing, while nine Jews did not! And all this, leads up to the Parable of the *"good Samaritan"* (Luke 10:30-37), which showed the Jewish priest and Levite in a very poor light compared to the Samaritan who came to the aid of a battered and bruised man by the roadside.

This brought out into the open what the Pharisees and scribes did not want to hear. It was exposing the darkness of the human soul. No one, other than the Lord, could have taken such high ground.

This was morality par excellence!

Remarkably, his enemies recognized his truthfulness, yet graciousness. When they were sent to arrest him, they returned without Him, proclaiming, *"Never man spake like this man"* (John 7:46).

The moral glory that shone from the Saviour silenced the most severe critics. It could not be otherwise for John, the beloved disciple and apostle, writing years later said, *"The Word became flesh and dwelt among us and we beheld his glory the glory as of the only begotten of the Father **full of grace and truth**"* (John 1:14).

While we never could attain to this level of excellence, we are nevertheless exhorted to emulate the Apostle Paul who spoke the *"truth in Christ"* (1 Tim. 2:7) .

Serving Our Own Generation

"David, after he had in his own generation served the counsel—purpose—of God, fell on sleep, and was laid unto his fathers" (Acts 13: 36 R.V.)

"Served the purpose of God"	**Spiritual Activity**
"In his own generation (day)*"*	**Sensible Adaptability**
"Fell asleep (died)*"*	**Solemn Responsibility**

SPIRITUAL ACTIVITY:

We have not only to believe in, but to know, that God **is** alive! In 1 Samuel 17:26, David, referring to Goliath, said, *"he hath defied the armies of the **living** God."* When challenging the giant, the shepherd boy was not in any doubt about the results, *"I come to thee in the name of the Lord of Hosts, the God of the armies of Israel."* As he stood apparently alone, God had the valley of Elah filled with His hosts and, in that knowledge, fought to deliver his people. We too, are in a warfare against great odds but *"greater is he that is in you than he that is in the world"* (1 John 4:4). This really means that in any service for the Lord the source of our strength is spiritual and unconnected with human ability and ingenuity. Indeed, in a different context, the apostle Paul tells us that, *"the foolishness of God is wiser than men, and the weakness of God is stronger than men"* (1 Cor. 1:25). Not only did David's action bring the scorn of the giant and the army of Israel but his astonished brothers looked on aghast at the apparently foolhardy and extremely dangerous drama that was unfolding before their eyes. As I write, I am reminded of what the Master said to His disciples when commissioning them. *"I send you forth as sheep in the midst of wolves"* (Matt. 10:16).

SENSIBLE ADAPTABILITY:

No doubt David, as he progressed in his service for God,

might have wished to live in better times. In the previous generation it is recorded that, *"Israel served the Lord all the days of Joshua... and had known all the work of the Lord, which he had wrought for Israel"* (Josh. 24:31). Such was not the case with David. For practically the whole of his life he served God from a position of human disadvantage. As mentioned above it began at home with his family and it intensified with his in-and-out experiences with King Saul. He suffered the treachery of his rebel son Absalom and the indignity of seeking refuge among the Philistines. His great ambition, to build a house for God, was denied him and left for his son Solomon. Hunted, harried and hated he might have wondered why God had chosen this generation for him! There was too the period of failure and gross sin which caused him to suffer a divine four-fold retribution in the death of four of his sons. Yet, through it all, as the Psalmist he demonstrated his underlying trust and faith in God, adapting his activities as circumstances dictated. His life and service can be summarized in the well known and loved Psalm 23. Even in the valley of the shadow of death, the Shepherd led, restored and comforted him. Many who read and reflect on these facts may think about their own calling and service for God, and from them take courage and strength to fulfil their ministry. In the Apostle's reference in our text to David's service it is worthy of note that there is no mention of his failures. Despite them and the great grief they caused him, he was and ever remained: *"a man after God's own heart"* (1 Sam. 13:14).

SOLEMN RESPONSIBILITY:

"When thy days are fulfilled thou shalt sleep with thy fathers, I will set up my seed after thee... and they kingdom shall be made sure for ever before thee; thy throne shall be established for ever" (2 Sam. 7:12-16). This prophecy has been fulfilled to the letter in David's greater son Messiah Jesus! The angel said to the startled maiden Mary, *"The LORD God shall give unto Him the throne of His father David... and of His kingdom there shall be no end"* (Luke 1:32-33). These remarkable events underline

the significant role that David had in the plan and purpose of God. He was not to know the full extent of it in his lifetime as we even in our generation cannot fully comprehend the wonder of God's matchless grace as He carries out His life in us. As with David there is an allotted span of service and specific areas of work given to us to fulfil and none of it is outside our God-given capacities. At the *bema* in a coming day the well worn lines will be borne out:

> Deeds of merit as we thought them,
> He will show us were but sin.
> Little acts we had forgotten,
> He will tell us were for him.

Sonship

*"As many as are led by the spirit of God, these are the **sons** of God"* (Rom. 8:14).

*"The Spirit himself witnesses with our spirits that we are the **children** of God"* (8:16, Revised Version).

Sons (*huios*) "expresses the dignity of the position into which the **child** is brought, and the character which is consistent therewith; **children** (*teknori*) is connected with the verb 'BEGET' and becomes effective in the New Birth" (W.E.Vine).

This concise explanation is of vital importance to an understanding of the difference between our **standing** in Christ as His children by faith. It is unconditional and permanent. Our relationship as sons however is the **state** or condition of our profession that confirms that we are truly His! That, as our text indicates, is true only in so far as *"we are led by the spirit of God."*

Quoting from the Revised Translation we note that the apostle John uses the word **children** on two occasions; *"But as many as received him to then gave he the right to be called the children of God, even to them that believe on his name"* (John 1:12), and in 1 John 3:1 we read; *"Behold what manner of love the Father hath bestowed upon us that we should be called children of God."* In both his Gospel and Letter the Apostle is concerned about *"life."* He states emphatically; *"These signs are written that ye may believe that Jesus is the Christ, the Son of God, and that **believing** ye may have **life** in his name"* (John 20:31). There must be a birth into God's family, and we enter as spiritual babies! The Apostle Peter expresses this truth beautifully; *"As newborn babes long for the spiritual milk which is without guile* (pure) *that you may grow* (nourished) *thereby unto salvation"* (1 Pet. 2:2). Kenneth Wuest has a helpful comment on this; "The word 'milk' here does not refer to that part of the Word of God which is in contrast to the meat or solid food as in Hebrews 5:13-14, but to the Word of God in general." There is a phrase in the Greek text not brought out in the translation: "resulting in your making progress in your salvation."

Before dealing with sonship it is important to note what the apostle Paul earlier in Romans 8 makes clear. The new or just born believer must quickly be taught that they have to deal with two conflicting principles, *"flesh"* and *"spirit,"* verses 8-13. A summary of these verses draws attention to the contrast between the *"old"* and the *"new"* sometimes referred to as *"the two natures."* *"Ye are **not** in the flesh"* (v. 9) is a reference back to our **standing** and by itself can cause the newborn to wonder why it is that they still continue to have trouble with the *"flesh."* The Apostle quickly clarifies this and removes any need for doubt by the use of two expressions; *"not in debt to the flesh"* (v. 12), and *"mortify the deed of the body"* (v. 13). As in Colossians 3:5; *"Mortify* [put to the death] *therefore your members which are upon the earth."* And in the subsequent verses to verse 17 he details the meaning and uses the picture of putting off the old and *"putting on"* the new!

Having traversed *"the new way of life"* thus far we now arrive at the high point of the apostles teaching regarding **sonship**; *"For as many as are led by the spirit of God, **these** are the sons of God"* (v. 14). If the maturing newborn is to be 'led', the obvious implication is one of willingness to be led. This is not a forced march! As in the early stages of human life, the young child must be taught respect for and obedience to parents, and that is not always easy to accept. Disobedience to the point of requiring chastisement does nothing to negate the **standing** of child to parent. There comes a point in the growing up where maturity sets in and the child accepts its **status** as one of listening and learning to follow the desires of the parent. In the spiritual realm this is the Apostle's argument; we could use the well-worn adage "like father like son"! So naturally the adolescent grows into an adult and the matter of leading is a delight with the unfolding of the deeper and richer things in life. So with the leading of the Spirit, the true privileges and responsibilities of sons is willingly taken on board. (It is perhaps unnecessary to state the obvious—that we are dealing with a generic term as with children, both male and female).

Dr. Octavius Winslow in his commentary on Romans Eight (1852), comments on this section of the chapter:

"The follower of the Holy Spirit can be certain that He knows where He is going and the destination to which He wishes to take us. He knows about the sunken rocks, the subtle snares and the satanic allurements and pitfalls. He understands the meaning of every groan, interprets the language of every sigh, He sees the tear and feels the pain. So He is ready at the right time and in the right place to administer His counsel. To check a miss demeanour, give a gentle rebuke, or tenderly whisper a promise resulting in the strengthening faltering steps."

And as He leads He encourages us to step out after Him. We might ask what kind of steps are we required to take? The Scriptures abound in these; there is a veritable staircase that winds ever onwards and upwards and as we ascend, the rarefied climate becomes a delight. We begin in measure to understand what the Apostle meant; *"But we all with unveiled face reflecting as a mirror, the glory of the Lord, are transformed into the same image from glory to glory, even as from the LORD the Spirit"* (2 Cor. 3:18).

Let us now conclude by listing three of the many steps that the Holy Spirit wishes us to take.

STEP 1:

To lead us **from ourselves** and our own ideas as to where we would be tempted to walk. We have already referred to the inclinations of the *"flesh"* in Colossians 3. We would do well to follow carefully the steps outlines by the Apostle in the journey from the *"old"* to the *"new."*

STEP 2:

To lead us **to Christ**; *"leaving you an example that you should follow his steps"* (1 Pet. 2:20-25). It has also been said that the word *"in"* relating to following is not there and for the fundamental reason that the Lord Jesus was sinless. The context here is *"suffering"* and many of the Lord's valiant labourers are serving Him in front line action. The promise for them is secure *"they that suffer* (endure) *for Him will one day reign with Him."* The Lord Jesus in His ministry to the disciples regarding the Holy Spirit said; *"He* (the Spirit) *shall not speak from Himself... He shall glorify Me; for He shall take of Mine, and shall declare it unto you"* (John 16:13-14). One other reference will suffice for this brief summary; *"As therefore ye received Christ Jesus the Lord, so walk in Him. Rooted and built up in Him, and stablished in your faith, even as ye were taught, abounding in thanksgiving"* (Col. 2:6).

STEP 3:

To lead us to **holiness**. 1 Corinthians 6:19-20 gives the basis upon which holiness to the Lord and His claim upon us is built; *"Do you not know that your body is a temple of the Holy Ghost which is in you, which ye have from God? and ye are not your own; for ye were bought with a price: glorify God therefore with your body."* The price paid in the coinage of heaven for our procurement was the vicarious suffering and death of God's beloved Son symbolised by the outpouring of His precious blood. As His possession then our response must be as hymnology puts it:

> Not that I have mine own I'll call,
>
> I'll hold it for the giver,
>
> My heart, my strength, my life, my all,
>
> are His and His far ever.
>
> —James G. Small

It has often been said that "God has a greater work to do in us than through us." His holiness **within**, outshining as His ambassadors **without!** The Holy Spirit wants to impress upon us that we are sanctified (set apart) as His chosen and special representatives to show to the world His love and His so amazing grace!

As we review our position both as **children** and **sons** (and there's so much more than mentioned in this brief study) we conclude with the Apostle in Romans 8:15-17; *"For ye received* *not again the spirit of bondage unto fear; but ye received the spirit of adoption, whereby we cry, Abba, Father. The spirit beareth witness with our spirit that we are the children of God: and if children, then heirs of God; and joint heirs with* **Christ.***"*

Stewardship

"And the Lord said, Who then is that faithful and wise steward, whom his lord shall make ruler over his household, to give them their portion of meat in due season?" (Luke 12:41).

"There was a certain rich man which had a steward; and the same was accused unto him, that he was wasting his goods. And he called him, and said unto him, What is this I hear of thee? Render the account of thy stewardship; for thou canst be no longer steward" (Luke 16:1-2).

"Let a man so account of us, as of ministers of Christ, and stewards of the mysteries of God. Here, moreover, it is required in stewards, that a man be found faithful" (1 Cor. 4:2).

Oikonomus, from which we derive our English word **economy**, has as its main meaning "good management" with the underlying obligation of "accountability." The Scriptures quoted above illustrate these basic principles. Stewards, in the context of Luke's account were trusted servants normally permanently employed or residing in the house. They usually were over the servants and responsible to their master for the proper running and order of the estate or house. They acted as agents and had full authority to transact business in the master's name. This latter aspect can easily be applied to the apostle Paul's ministry answerable as he was to the Master who called and commissioned him to be the bearer of the Gospel. He called himself an ambassador for Christ—a truly privileged and responsible position.

Dr. David Gooding, in his commentary on the Gospel of Luke, draws a very interesting and instructive comparison between the actions of the prodigal in chapter fifteen and that of the wasteful steward in chapter sixteen. The former "wasted his substance in riotous living," becoming destitute, while the steward in chapter sixteen wasted his master's resources and deceitfully sought to protect himself from future poverty. He cites the first parable as a marvellous illustration of the Gospel. The pardon and forgiveness the father gives is unqualified and extremely costly but given freely to his son. His position in the home was fully restored. The ring, the feast, the outpouring of love made up for all and more that he had selfishly and foolishly lost. All totally undeserved! On the other hand there were severe consequences for the wasteful steward's failure. He lost his job! And he tried to cover his tracks. The under-handed arrangements that he made with others who owed the master money, though disgraceful, were commended by his master for his foresight in securing friends for times of future wants. However, the Lord Jesus, in His summary, shows the eternal difference that will arise through unfaithful steward-ship; *"He that is faithful in a very little is faithful also in much; and he that is unrighteous in a very little is also unrighteous in much... If you have not been faithful in that which is another's, who will give you that which is your own? No man can serve masters.... Ye can-not serve God and mammon"* (Luke 16:10-13).

The message surely must be that there is no comparison between the passing and empty things of this world and the eternal riches that are reserved for those who honour and serve the best of Masters! In any event, what we have, even of value by this world's standards, is really not our own. We have it on trust and one day must yield it up. The apostle Paul, writing to Timothy, spells it out in stark reality: *"Godliness with content-ment is great gain. For we brought nothing into the world, for neither can we carry anything out"* (1 Tim. 6:6-7).

On the matter of accountability, the truths expressed above are augmented and reinforced by the Apostle when he refers to: *"every man's work shall be made manifest; for the day shall declare it, because it is revealed in fire; and the fire itself shall prove each man's work of what sort it is. If any man's work shall abide which he built thereon, he shall receive a reward. If any man's work shall be burned, he shall suffer loss but he himself shall be saved, so as by fire* [with difficulty]*"* (1 Cor. 3:10-15). Earlier in the chapter, the Apostle describes various types of building material. We do well to examine carefully and prayerfully the type of material we are building with.

Yes, we survey the past:
Chosen, not for good in me

Wakened up from wrath to flee,
Hidden in the Saviour's side,
By the Spirit sanctified.

We think of the present:
Teach me Lord on earth to show
By my life how much I owe.

—A.M. Toplady

What of the future?

"That ye may approve the things that are excellent; that you may be sincere and void of offence unto the day of Christ. Being filled with the fruits of righteousness, which are through Jesus Christ, unto the praise and glory of God" (Phil. 1:10-11).

The Bowed Head

"When Jesus therefore had received the vinegar, he said, It is finished; and he bowed his head and gave up his spirit" (John 19:30).

The bowing of the head was a significant act of total control. All around the Lord was confusion and mayhem. But He alone knew what was being accomplished. The original word for **bow** is *klino* and it will be helpful to look briefly at the other three references to this word in the New Testament.

1. *"Foxes have holes, birds have their nests, but the Son of Man has not where to **lay** (bow) his head"* (Luke 9:58).

This speaks of **homelessness**! John 1:12 speaks of Him coming to His own things and His own people not receiving Him.

> Wandering as a homeless stranger
> In the world His hands had made.
>
> —James G. Deck

But now fixed to this tree of unresting agony, the symbol of earth's rejection, He lays His head—a deliberate act—on His breast. For over thirty years He had been a white lily toiling within a morass of sin. Now, at last, the work of Redemption is complete; so He pillows His head and tells His spirit to be gone!

FINALLY HE IS AT REST

2. *"And they constrained him saying Abide with us: for it is toward evening, and the day is now **far spent** [the day is bowed]"* (Luke 24:29).

The sun has set, another day's labour has ended; the workman can now be at rest. What a marvellous picture of what was happening at that momentous moment on Golgotha. On crying **"accomplished,"** He demonstrated that:

HE FULFILLED HIS FATHER'S WILL

This is the high point in the death of Christ. He carried out the Divine commission to the letter. He fully told out the love of God for a lost world.

HE MET THE CLAIMS OF A BROKEN LAW

At every turn and in every age man had rebelled again God's holy law. The law demanded that the *"soul that sins would die."* Now in the work on the Cross as the day sets, He assumes the guilt of a broken law and suffers the penalty — **death**!

"He saved others, He cannot saved Himself," they taunted. But they never spoke truer words!

HE MADE RECONCILIATION POSSIBLE

The great truth of the atonement is that, as the Apostle Paul puts it, *"We are reconciled to God by the death of His Son"* (Rom. 5:10). God was never at a distance from us! We were the ones who needed to be brought near.

HE DESTROYED THE WORKS OF SATAN

There is no better commentary on this than the words of Scripture: *"He destroyed principalities and powers... and made a show of them openly"* (Col. 2:15).

"He destroyed him that had the power of death, that is the devil, and delivered them who through fear of death were all their lifetime subject to bondage!" (Heb. 2:15).

As the Saviour bows His head in death, these tasks — each of them awesome — have been **accomplished** so He **now** can rest!

3. Our final reference to *"klino"* is Hebrews 11. 34 *"...**turned to flight** [bowed] the armies of the aliens."*

THIS IS VICTORY!!

Mission accomplished; sin judged and the enemy of souls routed! He is now our **Lord Jesus** the **Christ.** *"The Captain* [pioneer] *of salvation, leading many sons to glory"* (Heb. 2:10). A pioneer is someone who does something that was never done before, someone who blazes the trail!

WITH VICTORY ASSURED HE BOWS HIS HEAD AND DISMISSES HIS SPIRIT

And when He comes in bright array,

And leads the conquering line,

It will be glory then to say,

That He's a friend of mine.

The Christian's Proclamation

"For the preaching of the cross is to them that perish foolishness; but unto us which are saved it is the power of God.... But we preach Christ crucified, unto the Jews a stumbling block , and unto the Greeks foolishness. But unto us which are called, both Jews and Greeks, Christ the power of God, and the wisdom of God" (1 Cor. 1:18, 23-25).

This is the day of **slogans** for every conceivable cause under the sun!

For the church, *"we preach Christ crucified"* is not a slogan, but a **proclamation**.

Many years ago, while travelling in the country on business, I stopped by a boarded up Wesleyan church. The fabric of the building peeped out between the ivy and the briars. Above the door a stone was partly visible with a date on it, and underneath I could just make out the words *"we preach."* The growth of years covered the rest!

There are many preaching all kinds of religions and creeds. But nothing is on a par with the preaching of **Christ crucified**. Today, it is a proclamation that is labelled "Fundamentalism," and attributed to that extreme right wing of the evangelical church which appears to the critics to have no other message!

We will appreciate why there is this emphasis when we reflect that **the cross of Christ**:

Demonstrates the depravity of the human heart;

Displays the love of God;

Describes the wickedness of man;

Divides all of humanity

Determines man's destiny;

Demands the denial of self (Luke 9:24-26).

It was the German theologian Eric Sauer, in his book *Dawn of World Redemption* who said that the Cross was of

All Ages the turning point
All Love the highest point,
All Suffering the deepest point,
All Salvation the starting point.

At the Cross, God substituted the Lord Jesus'
Sinlessness for my sinfulness,
Holiness for my unholiness,
Righteousness for my unrighteousness.
Purity for my impurity.

He gave **all** that He was for **all** that I am.

Hallelujah, what a Saviour!

The Good Shepherd
In Action

The central chapters of John's Gospel are interconnected and developed in an interesting way. The central theme is the activity of the Lord Jesus Christ as the Good Shepherd. This study follows His involvement in word and action as He establishes His credentials as the One sent to accomplish the Father's will by *"laying down His life and taking it up again."* We commence with the failure of the shepherds of Israel in chapter nine and conclude with the astonishing episode of washing His disciples' feet in chapter thirteen.

> *"The blind man answered and said, 'A man that is called Jesus made clay and anointed mine eyes, and said unto me, "Go to the pool of Siloam and wash," and I went and washed and received sight' ... Jesus heard that they had cast him out* [of the synagogue]; *and when He found him, He said unto him, 'Dost thou believe on the Son of God?'... and he said, 'Lord, I believe.' And he worshipped Him"* (John 9:11,36-38).

Here we have the story of a blind man who finds the Saviour and has his sight restored. Or we could say that he was a lost sheep in the fold of Israel, who is found by the **true** shepherd, John 10.1. The religious leaders of Israel did not recognize the voice of the True Shepherd. In fact, they accused Him of being false, *"they had agreed, already, that if any man would confess him to be the Christ the Messiah, he should be put out of* [excommunicated] *the synagogue"* (v. 22).

Instead of these shepherds of the nation recognising and rejoicing that one of their "sheep" had his eyesight restored, they put him out of the synagogue, disgraced and disowned. These religious leaders were more concerned with their traditions and status than with the Word of God. They assumed that they were pleasing God, while all the time their minds were closed to who Jesus really was. They saw their position as leaders of the Jewish flock threatened by the actions and teachings of the young rabbi from Nazareth.

But the excommunication of the newly sighted man from the synagogue led to him being found by the Good Shepherd who had just given him, not only physical sight but would give an even greater blessing, **spiritual sight**! When he met his benefactor face to face, he obviously did not recognize Him. He had met Him, heard His command *"Go wash,"* but couldn't see Him. And so he has to ask, *"Who is He that I might believe?"* What an unforgettable experience to hear the words, *"Thou has both seen Him and it is He that talketh with thee."* He was seeing for the first time the face of the Son of God, Messiah of Israel, and Saviour of the world!

The prophecy against the shepherds of Israel detailed in Ezekiel 34 is summarized in verse 4.

> *"The diseased have you not strengthened, neither have ye healed that which was sick, neither have ye bound up that which was broken, neither have ye brought again that which was driven away, neither have ye sought that which was lost, but with force and with rigour have ye ruled over them. And they were scattered because there was no shepherd."*

This story is a living parable. The thieves and robbers are direct references to the false shepherds who treated this man so disgracefully. In contrast, the heart of the Good Shepherd went out after this disfigured and sick sheep, giving him not only his sight but Life in abundance.

As we enter chapter 10 and listen to the familiar words, *"Verily, verily, I say unto you"* our first question is, Who is the Lord speaking to? The final words of chapter 9 give us the answer; *"...**your** sin remains."* So He is continuing to address the same people, the religious hierarchy of Israel, referred to above. He accuses them of an improper entry into the fold in contrast to His own entry by the door.

This is therefore a pivotal chapter. It introduces a dispensational change summarized in chapter 1:17. *"The law was given by Moses, but grace and truth came by Jesus Christ."*

The *"the door into the sheepfold"* (v. 1) is referring to the gate of a winter sheepfold. This was a communal enclosure in which a number of flocks were kept in safety during the long winter nights and was guarded by a gatekeeper, the "porter" also referred to as a *"hireling"* (v. 12). The shepherds would come for their flocks and be admitted by him. He obviously would open to the bona fide shepherds. The Lord was clearly signalling that He had the proper credentials to be admitted as the true Shepherd into the fold, which was Israel. The Old Testament Scriptures right from Genesis to Malachi abound in prophetic references to the coming of such a One. Details of His proper ancestry through the patriarchs, kings and prophets, the place and nature of His birth are all well recorded.

We might ask, in this context, Who is the porter? It seems He is referring to John the Baptist, the one who introduced the Shepherd to the nation as *"the Lamb of God."* As He emerges from the Jordan waters at His baptism the heavens are opened, the Spirit of God descends and authenticates His divine credentials *"This is My beloved Son in whom I am well pleased."*

As we move to verse 7, the Shepherd refers to another sheepfold door, not guarded by a porter but by Himself. It is a reference to the summer sheepfold—a stone pen, the entrance to which is an opening without a door. When night comes, the shepherd counts and inspects his sheep as they pass under the rod, Ezekiel 20:37. He lights a fire and then positions himself across the opening and becomes the door of the sheep. This Shepherd, however, lifts the natural to the supernatural and continues *"By Me if any man enter in he shall be saved and shall go in and out and find pasture."* He has come not only to bring security to the flock but liberty. He will do it by *"laying down his life for the sheep."* We grasp the pathos of this as He continues, *"Therefore doth My Father love Me because I lay down My life that I might take it again"*! This is a preordained agreement within the Godhead, planned from eternity. But not just for the salvation of Jewish sheep! True it was among them that the good news of eternal life would be preached first, as referred to in Matthew 10. 5-6, when commissioning His disciples *"go not into any way of the Gentiles… but go rather to the lost sheep of the house of Israel."* However He makes clear in this discourse (v. 16), *"other sheep I have which are not of this* [Jewish] *fold, them* [Gentiles] *also I must bring and there shall be one flock and one shepherd."* Note *"flock"* as opposed to *"fold."*

We need to pause here and contemplate the verb *"have"* that He uses for both sets of sheep. Twice over in verses three and four He calls His Jewish sheep *"His own,"* saying that He knows their names, that they will hear His voice and follow Him. The verb *"have"* indicates prior ownership, the divine plan of election. Four times over in the following Olivet discourse in chapter 17:6, 9, 11 and 24, He refers *"to those whom thou hast given Me."* It is well for us to remember that God is the first cause of our salvation and in chapter 6:44 we have this truth reinforced *"….no man cometh to Me except the Father which sent Me draw him."*

Verse 18 is the high water mark of this discourse. *"No one takes My life from Me, but I lay it own of Myself, I have power* [right/authority] *to lay it down, and I have power* [right/authority] *to take it again, this commandment have I received from My Father."*

What a statement! Unparalleled in all time and beyond human comprehension. In speaking out these words with all that they implied, the Good Shepherd signalled the way by which He would fulfil His Father's will expressed in the best known verse of Scripture. Let us marvel again at what it says *"For God so loved the world, that He gave His only begotten Son. That whosoever believeth in Him should not perish but have everlasting life"* (John 3:16).

The title of this study is, "The Good Shepherd in Action." So it is therefore not surprising that He now illustrates that He means what He says. How best can He demonstrate it? He allows the deepest sorrow and heartbreak to enter the little home in Bethany with an illness that led to the death of his close friend Lazarus. His sisters Mary and Martha were beside themselves with grief. *"Lord,"* they chided in succession, *"if thou hadst been here my brother had not died"* (11:21-32). The Good Shepherd's reaction is vividly described for us in verses 33-35 in three terse statements; *"he groaned in the spirit"; "and was troubled"; "Jesus wept."* To "groan" has the meaning of righteous anger even to the point of rage. Why so? What filled the Shepherd's gentle soul with indignation? As He stood outside that tomb, its mouth closed with a stone, He saw that the man, created by God His Father in His image, was now a rotting corpse, as the results of sin, and because of it death reigned. The man He lost in Eden now seemed to be more lost than ever, and not this man only but all before him and the generations to follow, *"born in sin and shapen in iniquity"* (Ps. 51:5). The arch enemy, the deceiver himself was responsible and that made the Good Shepherd exceedingly angry. This resulted in His *"being troubled."* This is the same expression used in John 5:4-7 regarding the "troubling" of the waters. When a calm pool is troubled it ripples, we might say it trembles. I have a firm conviction that as the Lord stood there, He literally trembled. Did He tremble because He knew all that was to befall Him: the horror of Gethsemane, the cruelty of Pilate's judgement hall, and above it all, the purpose for which He came to defeat him who had the power of death, pay the ransom price for man's redemption and meet the requirement of His Holy Father? Then the climax; Divine eyes shed human tears! It was but a foretaste of the *"strong crying and tears"* (Heb. 5:7) that were to be His lot. Amazingly He then cries with a loud voice after prayer to His Father: *"Lazarus come forth!"* (11:43). We might join in worship now with the hymn writer, R. Lowry, "Death could not keep its prey, Jesus my Saviour. He tore the bars away Jesus my Lord." This episode was a precious foretaste of the certainty of His own resurrection when He would become the first fruits of a mighty harvest.

It is not surprising therefore that we find the Good Shepherd as guest at the table of the united family in Bethany in chapter 12. What a reunion that must have been! For a visitor to that supper, who was not familiar with the previous events, to be told that the man Lazarus sitting there in perfect health and looking as he always had been, was in recent times dead and decaying for four days in a tomb, would have been extremely difficult to believe. But this is a demonstration, however limited, of what abundant life in Christ brings. Not only satisfying in the present but assurance of being like Him and seeing Him as He is for all eternity. Sinless and deathless. We listen to His own assurance, *"Because I live you shall live also."*

As we join in spirit in the celebrations in Bethany, we could say that it is not only a house of Feasting, but also a house of Favour—their Lord was present. This makes it too a house of Fellowship, full family relationships have been restored. But soon it would be a house of Fragrance! Let us observe it again as though we had been there; *"Mary therefore took a pound of ointment of spikenard, very precious. And anointed the feet of Jesus, and wiped His feet with her hair: and the house was filled with the odour of the ointment"* (v. 3). There is every possibility that John, the recorder of the incident, and the other disciples were present. We should note verse 2, *"...Lazarus was **one** of them that sat at meat with Him."*—a clear indication that others, unnamed were present. As they all eventually left the home that day, the fragrance that permeated their clothes would travel with them. This begs the question, How is it with us? Indwelt by the Holy Spirit, assured of the Lord's continual presence, are we spreading abroad the fragrances of love, gentleness and goodness, to mention but a few of the graces available to us, as we walk and work in a polluted world.

We conclude this study with a brief reference to chapter 13. In one sense we move from a consideration of the actions of the Good Shepherd to that of the Great Shepherd, (Heb. 13), demonstrating a foretaste of His present ministry; washing the feet of His disciples. Recently I have pondered the implication of verse 12, *"So when he had washed their feet..."* Twelve pairs of feet! How long it would take their Master to do this is uncertain, but possibly at least one hour, and on His knees! What devotion!

I wonder, too, what the inner thoughts of the disciples were as they waited their turn? We certainly know Simon Peter's reaction and the profound lessons we learn from it But what of Judas? It seems clear from the context that he had his feet washed. Perhaps as it took place he did not fully realize the full implications of what was to follow. It was only after receiving the sop (v. 27) that Satan entered into him and propelled him relentlessly to the betrayal of the One he had followed for over three years, and to suicide. What an awful end! From the intimacy of "heaven" in the upper room to the eternal darkness of a lost eternity.

Looking at this event, what practical lesson can we learn? We recognize that while the laying aside of His garments speaks of His humility and grace in incarnation, it surely directs our minds to the right hand of the Majesty on high where He ministers to us with intercession and advocacy. Intercession is for the "fail-ability" of our humanity and advocacy for when we sin and truly confess it. There is however the underlying truth of cleansing from the defilements of the way on a continuous basis. However we ask ourselves, what did their Master mean when he counselled, *"If I then your Lord and Master have washed your feet, ye also ought to wash one another's feet. For I have given you an example that ye should also do as I have done to you"* (vv. 13-14)? How can we in some way fulfil His command in this present day? The message can have lost nothing of its power and pathos over the centuries. And so as we reflect on all that He, the Great Shepherd of the sheep, has and is doing for us perhaps today and tomorrow, we could begin by picking up the telephone, writing and sending a letter, or knocking on a believer's door to do a little bit of "feet washing."

We must too, remember that one day soon He will appear as the Chief Shepherd (1 Pet. 5:4). That will be the consummation of all that He, in His grace, has called us to be and do for Him.

The Kind Of People God Uses

A MAN WITH FEAR IN HIS HEART

"Now the word of the Lord came unto me saying…. I have appointed thee a prophet unto the nations. Then said! Behold I cannot speak for I am a child" (Jer. 1:5-6).

Jeremiah was a man who knew his limitations and his feebleness for such a task. He lived to see the end of the Single Kingdom period, when Judah's last kings ruled. His main ministry was to bring God's warning to them of their sin and iniquity—the most difficult of difficult tasks. He was probably shocked at the call of God in his life. Perhaps as the implications dawned on him, fear gripped his heart and he remonstrated about his inability to be God's messenger.

The Lord's response to him was simple and unambiguous *"Be not afraid because of them, for I am with thee to deliver thee…. Behold I have put My words in thy mouth"* (Jer. 1:8-9). The truth of the matter is, whom God calls, He equips. Proverbs 29:25 tells us that *"the fear of man bringeth a snare."* Who has not looked over his shoulder to hear what is being said about him!

If the Lord *"puts words on our mouth"* we have no need to fear.

A MAN WITH FOUNTAINS IN HIS EYES

"Oh that my head were waters and my eyes a fountain of tears, that I might weep day and night for the daughters of my people" (Jer. 9:1).

This was a man who could, and was not afraid, to shed tears. He did not weep because of his own rejection by the people, but for their rejection and rebellion at not listening to the voice of God. Small wonder that he is called the "weeping prophet." Weeping day and night reminds us of the Apostle Paul in his last meeting with the elders from Ephesus *"Remember that by the space of three years, I ceased not to admonish everyone night and day with tears"* (Acts 20:31) and his great concern over the *"grievous wolves that would enter not sparing the flock."* One could almost say two hearts, in different circumstances and different eras, beat as one, men whose hearts God had touched.

What a lesson for this generation! As we approach the end of the age, our world was never more against God than it is now and there is an urgent need for the Church of God universally to weep over it.

A MAN WITH FIRE IN HIS BONES

"… there is in my heart, as it were, a burning fire shut in my bones" (Jer. 20:9).

Jeremiah is sore tried. He feels that the Lord has deceived him. He has been thrown into prison because of his severe words to the nation. Yet, in the midst of his despondency, he says, *"…but the Lord was with me as a mighty one"* (v. 11).

The burning fire in his bones was due to sheer frustration tearing at his heart. He was convinced that his persecutors would be *"made to stumble"* which would ease the pain of his burning breast. He had bared his soul to the Lord, (v. 12) and ended up singing His praises (v. 13).

This is a real word of encouragement to us to remember that however difficult involvement in the Lord's work becomes, He is labouring together **with** us (1 Cor. 3:9) He will never leave or forsake us, He will accomplish His work.

It is well to remember :

God has a greater work to do in us than through us.

The Ministry Of Giving

In 2 Corinthians chapters 8 and 9, we have the Church's **maintenance** and **movement, succour** and **support**. These are paragraphs of powerful appeal in a very sensitive letter. We gather from the apostle's letter to the Roman Christians (Rom. 15:25-27) and now to the church at Corinth, that he had told the believers in Macedonia (Northern Greece) and Achaia (Southern Greece) about the dire straits of the saints in Jerusalem and Judea through persecution and famine, and of their reaction, particularly of the three Macedonian churches: Berea, Thessalonica and Philippi. The apostle, in writing to the Galatian churches, refers to his visit to Jerusalem to acquaint the "pillars" of the church, Peter, James and John of the success of the Gospel among Gentiles. *"...And when they perceived the grace that was given unto me ... they gave me and Barnabas the right hands of fellowship, that we should go unto the Gentiles. Only they would that we should* **remember the poor***, which very thing I was also zealous to do"* (Gal. 2:8-10). However when he arrives at the Macedonian churches he discovers that they are extremely poor and it is very interesting to note how he deals with the situation in the context of the injunction given to him to *"remember the poor."*

The chapters before us give a detailed account of the events, reactions and results of that visit. They can be conveniently discussed under four headings as follows:

THE PLEA TO BE INVOLVED

We see in the opening paragraphs the twin streams of poverty and liberality flowing freely. When the Apostle saw their *"affliction"* and *"deep poverty"* (8:2) he no doubt would have in the forefront of his mind their own need of material help. Under the circumstances he might have argued that it wouldn't be reasonable to inflict on them the great need of the practical assistance required for the church Jerusalem. He would wait until he went south to the prosperous church in Corinth *"...that you come behind in no gift"* (1 Cor. 1:7) and get what was needed there. But it is clear that he told them the situation as it was. Why? Because he saw "giving" as a priestly ministry and part of the church's worship and he must not deny these believers this ministry, impoverished though they were. In this connection perhaps a practical comment is not out of place. When we meet as companies of believers to "remember the Lord" we should always consider that our "offering" is an integral part of the worship that we are rendering to Him. When they heard the report, they "beseeched" the Apostle to be involved and we learn the results of that: *"abounding unto the riches of their liberality, first they gave their own self to the Lord. For according to their power* [ability], *I bear witness, yea and beyond their ability they gave of their own accord"* (v. 5). We are given no clue as to the monetary amount that was collected, that is not the point; it was the heart, beating with love to their Lord and their brethren that motivated them to give.

As I consider these verses I have in my mind the situation in May 1984 in Sibiu, Romania. Four hundred believers, in boiling temperatures, crushed into an old factory building were listening to an account of the extreme famine conditions in Ethiopia. First there were tears, then sobs and finally audible cries (translated into) "What can we do to help?" We had come from the "West" with financial help for the suffering and impoverished Romanians, now we were privileged to see the Macedonian plea in action. Before we left an offering was taken for Ethiopia! Again I have no knowledge of the amount taken up. In their circumstances it not have been very large but the truth of this Macedonian example was being followed almost to the letter.

We cannot leave these paragraphs without reference to the greatest act of self sacrifice ever made, all human sacrifice fades and disappears at the profound words. *"For ye know the grace of our Lord Jesus Christ, that though He was rich , yet for your sakes He became poor that ye through His poverty might become rich"* (v. 9). There can be no doubt that it was **this** sacrifice and supreme example that inspired the Romanians and saints down the centuries, to give to those in need. This should be the basis of our giving to the Lord for His people and the maintenance of His work.

THE PRINCIPLES OF INVOLVEMENT

There are three elements in this :

"For if the **readiness** *is there…"* (v. 13). This is not a tax or an obligatory tithe. Yet it would appear that there is a carry over from Exodus 35.21-22, *"And they came … everyone whom his spirit made willing and brought the Lord's offering."* If there is a willing mind, the rest is easy. If there is no willingness, it really is not worth giving at all. This has echoes of the "widows mite." For her it was a willing act of dedication to God The commendation of the Lord gives significance to this ministry of giving. This the apostle also underlines; *"Let each man do according as he hath purposed in his heart; not grudgingly, or of necessity* [not obligated] *for God loveth a cheerful giver"* (ch. 9:7).

"According as a man **hath***,"* not according as he hath not. It is quality God is interested in not quantity. God does not ask any of His children to give what they do not have. Such an exercise before God would undoubtedly lead to a reassessment of one's lifestyle. Sometimes we sing too casually:

> Not that I have mine own I call,
>
> I hold it for the Giver,
>
> My heart, my strength , my life, my all,
>
> Are His and His for ever.

I recall a brother in my own assembly saying on one occasion, "We may not speak lies but sometimes we sing them!" I have never forgotten that.

"That others may be eased and you not distressed, but by **equality***…"* is the third element. God is looking for fairness and an even burden of stewardship laid upon his people. The believers in Jerusalem by this principle would accept the gift and have their distress eased. But as we shall see later it was not a one-way exercise. What the saints in Jerusalem lacked materially was made up by them to their Gentile brothers and sisters in a spiritual way. The Lord truly is no man's debtor.

A PRACTICAL EXAMPLE OF INVOLVEMENT

"But thanks be to God, which put the same earnest care for you into the same into the hear of Titus ... but being himself very earnest, he went forth unto you of his own accord" (v. 16). The zeal of Titus was the spontaneous action of a heart touched with the love of Christ. Note the steps that led him to take this journey south to Corinth,

> He heard of the need: *"... the earnest care for you"*(v. 16).
>
> He paid attention to what he heard: *"accepted our exhortation"* (v. 17).
>
> He received the Apostle's commendation: *"...he is my partner, my fellow worker"* (v. 23).
>
> He put his exercise into practice: *"....he went forth of his own accord"* (v. 17).

I believe the force of this last comment is that he "paid his own way," whereas the two brethren that accompanied him were sent by the churches and possibly had their expenses paid! Titus was prepared to spend and be spent, not only out of respect for the apostle but for his Master. As far as he was concerned, understanding of the plight of his fellow Christians in Jerusalem and ensuring that they got the help they needed was paramount and all the more remarkable because of their Jewish background!

THE PURPOSE OF THE INVOLVEMENT

In the latter part of chapter 9, the apostle shows that there is a three dimensional aspect to this ministry. First of all there is (as mentioned above) the material supply going East. Then we see secondly that there is a reciprocal spiritual supply coming West! *"Seeing that through the proving of you by this ministration, they* [the Jerusalem saints] *glorify God for the obedience of you confession unto the Gospel of Christ and for the liberality of your contribution.... While they themselves also, with supplication on your behalf, long after you by reason of the exceeding grace of God in you"* (vv. 13-14). The word *supplication* carries the meaning of beseeching or longing for. The prayers of the church at Jerusalem were focused and intense and, as I have said, all the more remarkable because their objects were Gentiles. It assures us of the work of the Holy Spirit underscoring the reality of One Body.

Perhaps I can refer in this connection to another experience I had at a meeting in an isolated Romanian Assembly near the Ukrainian border in 1987. The brother who led the meeting asked me at the close if I was an American! I said "No. I come from Northern Ireland." He said to me "That's where they do the bombing!" I was stunned and before I could say anything he continued, "I didn't know there were any Christians in Northern Ireland!" So, totally taken aback, I told him there were thousands of believers just the same as them in this village. With an earnestness which was tangible he the said, "You have brought to us today many helps for which we are very grateful, and now that we know that there are Christians in Ireland we will pray for them every day." Immediately I thought as I put my arm around him, "This is 2 Corinthians 8 and 9 in action."

But marvellous though this is, it pales into insignificance when we consider the third dimension; we could call it the Vertical one! God Himself is involved and so is His beloved Son. *"For the ministration of this service not only filleth up the measure of the wants of the saints, but aboundeth also through many thanksgivings to God, Seeing that the proving of you by this ministration they glorify God."*

Just as God is the first cause in salvation in which we see the glory of His grace, we now go a step further and see that glory manifested in the togetherness of ethnic opposites who are now one in Him, resulting in added glory. Then too we must pause, as we close this study, to consider the last verse of this chapter, *"Thanks be to God for his unspeakable* [inexpressible] *gift"* (v. 15). I have no doubt that this is a direct reference to the Father's love gift – His beloved Son and the infinite cost paid for the redemption of those He has chosen from before the foundation of the world.

The Mystery Unveiled

"Having made known unto us the mystery of his will... to gather together all things in Christ, the things in the heavens and the things upon the earth; in him, I say" (Eph. 1:9-10).

We should note that *"heavens"* are properly in the plural (RV). They encompass not only our solar system, gigantic though it be, but the outermost reaches of God's creation, too vast for the greatest scientist, using the most advanced equipment, to measure let alone comprehend. The reference to the *"earth"* in the singular marks it out as unique among the multiplicity of the heavenly bodies.

The fact is, that it was on this tiny planet that God created and placed mankind. In time, this culminated in the greatest event in human history: the incarnation, life, death, resurrection and ascension of Jesus Christ our Lord.

We can but bow as we listen to the Apostle Paul, *"Great is the mystery of godliness, God was manifest in flesh"* (Tit. 3.16).

But the story is far from complete as the same Apostle declares in our Scripture. The plan will continue to unfold in the future. *"All things"* — animate and inanimate will be *"gathered together in Christ."* This expression (KJV) is a complex one having more than one root. It can come from the idea of "head" or "sum" and also "reversal." So commonly, a translation is to "head or sum up" and from another root the thought of "bring back or restore." We shall presently see how both can be harmonised.

First, follow the definition of restoration in the context of the heavens and the earth. This points back to a previous condition where no separation between the Creator and the created existed, back to the beginning when God was in harmony with all that He had made. He declared it to be *"very good"* (Gen. 1:31). The inspired Apostle contemplates a restoration to that former condition in the heavens and on the earth. The material universe, cursed by sin, will be brought back to its pristine state.

How will it be accomplished? It will commence with Messiah's millennial reign and culminate in the new heavens and earth (Rev. 21:1-5), wherein righteousness will dwell and all traces of the fall will be removed. Our Lord Jesus Christ will come again to *"receive the kingdom"* (Luke 19:15).

Think now of the idea of "heading up." He will be the summation and the centrepiece of God's final purpose and plan. There will be no other. Truly all *"the fullness of the Godhead"* will be revealed in the glorious Son of God as He is proclaimed:

King of kings and Lord of lords.

The Place Of The Skull

"When they were come to a place called Golgotha, that is to say, the place of a skull... there they crucified Him, and parted His garments, casting lots: that it might be fulfilled which was spoken by the prophets, 'they parted my garments among them, and for My vesture did they cast lots'" (Matt. 27:36).

Golgotha: the place of the skull. A scull has no brains. There seemed no rhyme or reason for the death of the Lord Jesus Christ. It was a mindless act and would have remained so had it not been revealed to us that *"He was delivered by the determinate counsel and foreknowledge of God"* (Acts 2:23).

Golgotha, for everyone except the Saviour, was a place of confusion and mystery. Pilate, the centurion, the soldiers, the woman, the disciples and those ordinary citizens of Jerusalem that "wagged their heads" as they went on their way, all in their own way, wondered.

They **wondered** about the cries from the cross, beginning and ending with *"Father"*!

That speaks of relationship! The Father was with Him through it all. He never forsook His Son. Hence, the mystery surrounding the central cry, *"My **God**, My **God** why hast **Thou** forsaken **Me**?"* It was God, the Holy and the Just, who turned His face from the sin of the world, of all ages, now laid upon the Sin Offering.

They **wondered** at the cry of strength and triumph. After a night and part of a day of horrendous torture, to cry with a LOUD voice *"finished"*! — **accomplished** — was mystery beyond words. It signalled the **completion** of the greatest act of all time, *"When He put away sin by the sacrifice of Himself"* (Heb. 9:26). If confusion reigned in the hearts and minds of all around Him, there was nothing but majestic control in this great act. In the prime of manhood, He hands over His spirit. He sends it away to His Father. He bows His head and is actively involved in the giving up of His life. We must ever remember that it did not take six hours for Jesus to die! His death was not a process; it was an **act**. He gave His life! *"No man,"* He said—not even

Caesar's soldiers—*"taketh My life from Me, I have power* [authority] *to lay it down and I have authority to take it again, this commandment have I received of My Father"* (John 10:18).

This is precisely what he did. His death was **vicarious, substitutionary**, **sacrificial** and **voluntary**, and for **all** who believe.

The Precious Promise

"Let not your heart be troubled... In My Father's house are many mansions... I go to prepare a place for you. And if I go ... I will come again, and receive you unto Myself; that where I am, there ye may be also" (John 14:1-3).

He is coming to fulfil a promise to His own **and** He never breaks His word.

Where is He now? He is in heaven at *"the right hand of the majesty on high"* (Heb. 1:3). His manhood is now glorified. He has truly gone away, and so now we await the fulfilment of His promise to return. In the interval, He has not left us in a vacuum. He has given us the Holy Spirit to indwell and He expects us to be occupied in His service. He expects us to watch and wait, and watch and pray.

While it was to His disciples, true sons of the patriarchs, that He made the promise, it is quite clear from the Shepherd discourse that He anticipated **other** sheep who were not of the Jewish fold. *"Them also,"* He said, *"I must bring and there shall be one fold* [**flock**] *and one shepherd"* (John 10:16).

From God's standpoint, this flock is a thing of exquisite beauty, and when He returns it will be seen to be so. *"He will present it to Himself a glorious church without spot or wrinkle"* (Eph. 5:27). Here we learn that He is going to **present** the church as a glorious thing. All the redeemed will be placed alongside Him for eternity!

> Let all who look for hasten
> The coming joyful day,
> By earnest consecration
> To walk the narrow way.
> By gathering in the lost ones
> For who our Lord did die,
> For the crowning day that's coming
> By and by.

The Prophetic Background
To The Gospel

In the Old Testament God gave the gospel to His called out people the Israelites in symbolism. The Tabernacle itself, in type together with the offerings and sacrificial systems, charted the way whereby man in his fallen nature could approach the God he had so blatantly sinned against. However, the prophetic nature of the Gospel goes back to the Edenic paradise. For, in symbol, the Cross, the heart of the Gospel, was erected at its gates, with a trail of blood that developed into a great and mighty river pointing forward to the ultimate shedding of the blood of God's beloved Son. The New Testament revelation states that, *"Once in the end of the age He* [Jesus, Son of God] *appeared to put away sin by the sacrifice of Himself"* (Heb. 9:26).

In the beginning we hear the Creator address the man and the woman whom He had created in His own likeness and for His own glory. *"Of every tree of the garden thou may eat freely eat but of the tree of the knowledge of good and evil thou shalt not eat of it; for in the day that thou eatest thereof thou shalt surely die"* (Gen. 2:17).

We might be tempted to ask why the Creator imposed such a restriction. It was because of the nature and composition of the beings he had created. The two dominant features given to them were intelligence and free will and in order for these to operate to their full potential they had to be tested. To obey or disobey was the test. They disobeyed!

This leads to the source of the disobedience; *"Now the serpent was more subtle than any beast of the field that the Lord God had made. And he said unto the woman. 'Yea, hath God said…'"* (Gen. 3:1). Yes He had. Now she was presented with the satanic test: *"ye shall **not** surely die!"* (v. 4). What would she do? She believed the serpent; she ate; she *"gave to he husband and he did eat and their eyes of them both were opened, and they knew that they were naked"* (v. 7).

Disrobed, dishonoured and disgraced through disobedience they were driven from the tree of life. The Apostle Paul describes their condition as *"dead in trespasses and sins"* (Eph. 1:1).

What would the Creator do now? *"And the Lord God made for Adam and his wife coats of skin and clothed them"* (Gen. 3:21). Where did the skins come from? Innocent animals! And blood had flowed! What is so significant about this? It is explained by God through the writer to the Hebrews 9:22: *"Without the shedding of blood is no remission* [forgiveness]*."* Here we have the basis of the everlasting Gospel and it is linked to the first profound prophetic statement in Genesis 3:15; *"I will put enmity between thee* [the serpent, the devil] *and the woman."* Her name is Eve, the mother of **all** living. And *"...between thy seed and her seed; it shall bruise they head and thou shalt bruise his heel."* That is the forecast of the satanic intervention at Calvary and divine overcoming and victory, The Messiah, the Christ there: *"destroyed him who had the power* [authority] *of death, that is the devil; and delivered them who through fear of death were all their lifetime subject to bondage"* (Heb. 2:15).

The Record Of The First & Last Great Apostasies

Apostasy: Is made up of two Greek words *apo* **"away from"** and *statis* **"standing"**, that is, "Standing away from God."

In Genesis, the book of **beginnings** and **seed plot** of the Bible, there are three major events of great importance:

1. **Creation**: The beginning of all earth-bound creatures and things.
2. **The Flood**: The alteration of the topography, geology and geography of the Earth.
3. **Babel**: The commencement of the races and languages of humans.

Also, it can be said that in Genesis **Babel** was the second great act of disobedience, the first being the fall of man in the garden of Eden.

In Genesis 8:15-17 and 9:1, Noah and his family, along with the entire contents of the **Ark**, have just set foot on a purged earth. This family were the only survivors of a dreadful world wide flood, which lasted for over a year and totally changed the topography of planet Earth.

They left the **Ark** with the clear command of God to, *"Bring forth......and* **multiply upon the earth***"* (8:17), *"Be fruitful and* **replenish the earth.***"* It was the Creator's intention that they would voluntarily multiply in numbers over the years and scatter to various parts of the earth, with His blessing (9:1).

At a cursory reading of Chapter 10, it would seem that is what they did. Verses 5, 20 and 31 read, *"These are the sons of Japheth—Ham—Shem … after their families, after their tongues, in their lands, in their nations."* It comes as a surprise and a puzzle when we read Chapter 11:1, *"Now the earth was of **one** language and **one** speech* [dialect]*!"* However the problem is not as great as it first appears. We know that the Scriptures are not written in strict chronological order and this does not apply only to the order of the Books of the Bible as we shall see when we come to consider **the last great apostasy** detailed in Revelation 13, 17 and 18.

In order that we make sense, then, of chapters 10&11 we conclude that the events of chapter 11 **precede** the events of chapter 10. The reason for this will become apparent later. To summarize the position we could say that: Chapter 11 is **why** God did what He did and Chapter 10 is **what** He did.

Let us now consider the dramatic events of chapter 11.

"As they journeyed east, they found a plain in the land of Shinar and they dwelt there" (v. 2).

The significant word here is **dwelt**. It means to "settle down." This is a **flagrant refusal to carry out the command of God** to keep on the march, to spread out, to promote the pioneering spirit demanding rigour, hardship, and insecurity. They were not prepared for this. The "plain in the land of Shinar" was too tempting, too alluring; they had travelled far enough. On the way, over the months and years they were multiplying. They all spoke the same language, all had the same desire, their leaders were all of the same mind. This was a good place to stay and build their society. Their main ambition was **the search for social security and wellbeing**. They distrusted the governmental command of God. They would seek comfort in their own desires and follow their own instincts. This was the first fatal step in their rebellion against God.

Shinar or Chaldea, later to be called Babylonia, was in the vast delta at the confluence of the great rivers Tigris and Euphrates, the border area of present day **Iraq** and **Iran**. This area has been identified as the eastern end of the **"Fertile Crescent"**, the area we now call the **Middle East** stretching in an arc-like shape from the Mediterranean Sea in the West. This ancient cradle of civilization has endured and remains in the present era a place of dominant world importance and attention.

It is the contention of the writer that this area will also be the theatre of **the last great apostasy** referred too, in summary, in Psalm 2. It is therefore, of vital importance that we pay attention to what Scripture has to say about these two great events.

If we are looking for a Biblical application of this, we need not look far. Human disobedience against God is **sin** and that is the all too often recurring theme of the Scriptures. Isaiah's words (out of context) sums it up, *"All we* [humanity from Eden until the final judgement] *like sheep, have gone astray, we have turned **everyone to his own way."***

The modern idioms: I will do it my way, do my own thing, everything is relative, there are no absolutes, no **right** or **wrong**, sum up modernity. Yes, it all began in the Garden of Eden, but at Shinar it is tragically repeated **and** advanced.

The welfare state that Western Society has enjoyed and will gradually creep across Europe (note the impending enlargement of the European Union) is nothing new. Ease of life and luxurious living has been the characteristic of many in society and usually at the expense of the poor and helpless. Even those in poverty and deprivation have it as a goal in their hearts to one day be rich!

INSTALLATION OF COMBINED INDUSTRY

"And they said one to another..." (v. 3).

What was about to take place did not happen by accident or on the spur of the moment. The decision they were about to take was the result of an agreed plan of action. This was nothing short of a **conspiracy** against God's command.

"Go to, let us make brick and burn them thoroughly, and they had brick for stone and bitumen for mortar."

Whatever it was they had in mind to build, it came from the careful planning and preparation of a strategy that would satisfy their selfish and Godless ideals. They must pool their energies and cooperate in labour. The materials they would use and how they would make them would give expression to the permanency of the venture. They were determined to make a good job of it. This was no half-hearted or haphazard adventure. It would be the glory of their diligence and expertise.

THE FORMATION OF A CONFEDERACY

"And they said, Go to let **us** *build* **us** *a city and a tower, whose top may reach unto heaven."* In the English translation the words *"may reach"* are in italics, they are omitted in the original text. The general consensus translation is *"like the heavens"* (v. 4).

They would build the city for accommodation and commerce. The building of a city we could accept as the normal and logical development of any new civilization. It is nothing less than what we would expect. Our interest, however, is aroused in respect of the building of the tower. What was it and what was it for?

In Genesis 1.14 the Creator had placed *"lights in the firmament of the heaven … and let them be for* **signs.***"* Jeremiah 10:2 refers to the same phenomena, *"Learn not the way of the nations and do not be dismayed at the signs of the heavens... for the nations were dismayed at them."* These references are relevant to our present study. The planners and builders of the tower were not so naïve as to try to build a tower that would reach literally to heaven. No, it was a carefully crafted high ideal; it was to **initiate their own religion** and **without God.**

The object of their worship would be the stars. This tower would be adorned with the signs of the heavens. There seems to be support for this understanding when we consider the references in 2 Kings 21:3; 23:5 and Job 38:2. The Kings passages refer to *"worshipping the starry hosts"* or the "signs of the Zodiac" as another translates it. In Job it is called the *"Mazzaroth"* which when translated means "the twelve signs."

This is, in effect, the commencement of Astrology. *Astro* means star; *ology* means doctrine. Worship of the stars.

This however was not a one way experience. There is ample evidence that there are astrological powers which influence human affairs. We have scientific knowledge of the moon and its relation to the seasons and its effects on the tides. But astrology goes farther and amounts to a Satanic working on humans as they expose themselves to the influences of the Zodiac.

Someone once said, "God put **His** signs in the sky for His glory, but the Devil created a counterfeit to thwart the purposes of God."

In many societies today the influences of astrology are all to apparent. The horoscope which gives people star signs and predictions on which they base their lives, together with palm reading, tarot cards and all similar forms of wizardry are tools of the occult.

A common saying is to "thank your lucky stars." The occult is not a **trivial fiction but a serious fact**. We must treat it as such.

GODLESS SELF-CENTREDNESS

*"Let **us** make **us** a name …"* (v. 4).

Now we get to the core of the devilish scheme. In verses 3 and 4 the word "**us**"is used four times! This truly was the exaltation of man's will over that of the Creator! It is the manifestation of **godless self centredness**. They wanted to make a **name** for themselves.

The original meaning in the Hebrew of "name" is *shem*. This is significant.

In Chapter 9:26, there is a special blessing pronounced by God on the line of Shem,

"Blessed be the Lord the God of Shem." So in effect, the inhabitants of Shinar were saying: If God has given a special blessing to the line of Shem let **us make us a** *shem*! We will bypass God's way. We will imitate God.

OPEN REBELLION

"Lest we be scattered upon the face of the whole earth" (v. 4).

God's desire, indeed, command, was to "**multiply**", "**be fruitful**", "**replenish**." But the people had other ideas. History has proved that, so far as man is concerned, there is **strength in numbers**. Mankind hates to be singled out or be alone. The establishment of confederacies, unions and the like find their origins at Shinar. Every such association has a motto or a badge and the badge of this Godless society was a satanic **tower**.

DIVINE INTERVENTION

*"And the Lord said, behold they are one people and they have all one language and this is what they begin to do and now nothing will be withheld from them, which they purpose to do. Go to, let **us** go down and confound their language, that they may not understand one another's speech"* (vv. 6-7).

Now it is God's turn to use the Divine and only authoritative **us**. The plurality of Deity! Some may originally have wondered why their activities provoked so much interest in heaven. It must be said that this was the greatest crisis in earth's history since the flood and if God's plan for the redemption of a fallen world was to be carried through then this devilish scheme must be stopped. Direct intervention was essential. It had to be sudden and decisive.

"So the Lord scattered them upon the face of the earth and they left off to build the city" (v. 8).

What God, in His providence, had asked them to do voluntarily, he now forces them to do against their instinct and wish. Note that the reference to ceasing to build applies only to the city! That was a very major and long term task. There is no mention of them ceasing to build the tower. The probability is that they finished it and were practising idolatrous worship in it when the judgement fell!

"Therefore was the name of it called Babel..." (v. 9).

It has been reliably stated that Bab-el means the **gate to God**. The scheme they had devised, so daring and far reaching in its design that would secure their future prosperity and peace has now been reduced to **confusion**. And the very thing they had engineered to avoid had happened.

Galatians 6:7 could be written over Babel, *"Be not deceived,*

God is not mocked, whatsoever a man sows that shall he also reap."

We have discussed the **why** of God's action and we now want to look at the implications of the **how** in Chapter 10:8-10. *"And Cush begat **Nimrod**, he began to be a mighty one in the earth. He was a mighty hunter before the Lord, wherefore it is said Like Nimrod a mighty hunter before the Lord. And the beginning of his kingdom was Babel… in the land of Shinar."*

This connection between Nimrod and Babel is significant. We have seen that the events of Chapter 11 precede those of chapter 10 so the idolatrous development of chapter 11 produces the world's first great dictator. The system produces the man and not the other way round as we might have thought. This is relevant and important when we come to consider the development of the **last great apostasy**.

Nimrod's name means "rebellious panther" and "the **lawless** one" The reference to Nimrod being a mighty hunter **before** the Lord, is more accurately translated **against** the Lord. He was not a hunter of animals but of men! All this is not surprising when we consider the environment in which he was reared and educated—Babel in the land of Shinar. The fact that he was the grandson of Ham indicates that his upbringing did not have a good beginning.

*"And he **began** to be a mighty one in the earth"* (v. 8).

This indicates a gradual process from obscurity to prominence and popular acclaim as a leader. The expanding Shinar population with all its aggressiveness was an ideal environment for the nurturing of this young man who through intrigue and ruthlessness would rise above his peers and ultimately take charge of all that Babel was and stood for.

The extra-biblical record of Nimrod tells us that the "**son of Cush**," was **Bar-Cush**, became corrupted to Bacchus (called the Lamented one). Historically Nimrod was known as **Ninus** (the **son**) His wife **Semiramus** was worshipped as the goddess **Rhea** (the **mother**). From this historians deduce that this was the beginning of the **mother** and **son** worship. The husband Ninus became synonymous with the **son** called by another name **Tammuz**. Ezekiel 8.14: *"behold there sat woman weeping for Tammuz"*(Read the context).

In support of the **mother** and **child** worship we know that:

Egypt: **Isis** and **Orisis**.

India: **Isi** and **Iswari**.

Italy: **Venus** and **Cupid**.

Rome: **Baal** and **Beltis**. (**Beltis** translated from Latin is *My Lady*. Italian is *Mea Domina*. [**Madonna** and **Child**]).

The **Child-Tammuz** was worshipped as a **god**.

Another translation of **mother** is **Juno** or **"queen of heaven."**

Jeremiah 7:18 *"woman kneads dough and make cakes to the queen of heaven."*

44:15-19 *"...the word that has gone forth to burn incense to the queen of heaven"; "and when we burned incense to the queen of heaven."*[1]

The vision that the prophet Ezekiel saw in Chapter 8 was in the **House of God**, the place where God in all His holiness said He wanted to reside.

" *...When the priests came out of the holy place, that the cloud filled the house of the Lord, so that the priests could not stand to minister by reason of the cloud, for the glory of the Lord filled the house of the Lord"* (1 Kings 8:10-11).

The place that once was filled with the presence and glory of the Lord is now filled with the abominations of devilish worship (Read Ezek. 8:1-18). And all finds its origin at Babel.

We know, of course that Babel, became Babylonia/Babylon. Its greatness and magnificence is described for us in history

---

1   Many commentators point to these Scriptures as referring to the Roman Catholic system and its head (the **Pope**) as the ultimate **lawless** one (**Antichrist**). This will be discussed when we come to consider the **last great apostasy**.

and is the subject of Daniel 1-4. There we are introduced to its wealthy lifestyle and great despotic ruler Nebuchadnezzar

"Thou O king are king of kings … thou art the head of gold" (Dan. 1:37-38).

"Is not this great Babylon which I have built for the royal dwelling place,by the might of my power and the glory of my majesty" (4:30).

As with Babel and their desire to make a **name**, so with Nebuchadnezzar. He was struck down as the dream (4:24-25) said he would be. God's judgement upon him came until he recognized that *"the Most High rules in the kingdoms of men."*

At the conclusion of chapter 5, we have the record of the capture of Babylon by Darius the Mede. He allied himself to Cyrus king of Persia, referred to in the **image** of chapter 2 as *"the breasts and arms of silver."* However, Babylon as a city remained for many years, it was not suddenly destroyed.

Many Bible students link the **fall** of Babylon as described in Daniel with its **destruction** as detailed in Isaiah chapter 13-14 and Jeremiah 50. However, when we consider Isaiah 13:9-13, we have reference to *"the day of the Lord"* in which end time events are referred to. To other students this indicates that the **total** demise of Babylon is yet future and that its **ultimate** end is described in Revelation chapter 18 which we shall discuss shortly.

It should also be pointed out that the characteristics of all four empires detailed in Daniel chapter 2 will be manifested in the end times in the **ultimate** "Babylon" system and city.

We now proceed to a consideration of the vision the prophet Zechariah had which lends support to this latter view.

This vision from Zechariah 5:8-11 is one of considerable importance because it has a direct link with the land of Shinar.

Here the prophet is taught that the influences directing nations would eventually find its permanent residence there. He was shown, not a sword, the symbol of warfare and conquering by fighting, but an **ephah**—the symbol of **commerce**.

"What is this that is going forth"—it had not reached its final destination, "this is the resemblance, through **all the earth**."

Note the global connection. When we come to consider what we mean by "**earth**" in Revelation, saying it primarily refers to the Roman world, there can be no doubt that no nation will be unaffected by **end time** events. From the Americas in the west to Japan in the East, none will be exempt.

Commerce—the need for economic prosperity, will be the characteristics of these times. Nations welcome it (e.g the enlargement of the European Union). Wars eat up economic resources and in the coming times mankind, weary with fighting, will welcome times of prosperity that the last great dictator—**antichrist**—will champion. There is still much brutality and "wars and rumours of wars" still persist, but they go hand-in-hand with international trade which will precede a time of unrivalled prosperity. The ephah is on the move but not yet reigning supreme.

Commerce and trade gives scope to man's entrepreneurial skills and energies. It stimulates research, equalises tariffs, ennobles science, promotes art and leisure. It is the answer to the world's problems. Who can blame the **ephah** for being anything but good?

"A woman seated in the middle of the ephah" (v. 7). A woman, in this connection, as we shall see later, symbolises a moral system, something that is outwardly attractive.

"this is wickedness"—**lawlessness**. It is the word that was attached to **Nimrod**, and is particularly used by the Apostle Paul in 2 Thessalonians chapter 2 as describing Antichrist. This lawlessness will not reach its full potential until it is established in the land of Shinar, (a literal geographical location) **back to the cradle of civisilation where it was so powerfully manifested and where it was judged.**

Lawlessness, as depicted in the vision, was **hidden**. When we come to consider its development in the **end times** we shall see it fully manifested.

The problem with **all** that is good in **commerce** is that intrinsic to it is the principle of evil eating away at honesty and integrity. All kinds of falsehood and deception permeate society in every nation and stratum of society in an increasingly open and aggressive way. Truth among governments and great trade organisations is in short supply (e.g. **Enron**).

"Two woman… with the wind in their wings… of a stork" (v. 9).

A possible reference to the dual role that the Civil and Religious powers will be working in concert (corruption is also manifested in many religious systems).

The stork is the strongest bird in flight and aided by the "wind" —unimpeded progress to the place of destiny.

"To build a house for it ….set it on its own base…in the land of Shinar" (v. 11).

It is very difficult to see any other meaning than the progress of the "stork" is nearing the end of its flight. It also means that there is an increasing shift of **commercial** supremacy from West to East (in the context of the Roman world). Note that the European Union, not USA, is the largest economic unit in the world! What destroyed the World Trade Centre in New York?— influences from the East!!

The stock market crisis is deepening in the West, while the East controls over two thirds of the world's oil resources.

This then is the record (in brief) **of the commencement and progress of the first great apostasy. We now look forward to where it is taking us.**

The Last Great Apostasy

We are now ready to look at some of the important issues that surround the **lawless one—the man of sin—the beast—antichrist** (all names and descriptions of the same person) as detailed in the New Testament.

Before this, perhaps it is necessary to say from which aspect we will endeavour to interpret Revelation chapters 13, 17, 18 and 19. There are others, strongly held, from the one I favour and pursue in the following pages. However in the matter of prophecy it is well to be careful; dogmatism is something that we must avoid at all times.

Some commentators view the section between chapters 6 and 18 as linear and chronological. I understand them better as a series of concentric circles—separate visions, each complete in themselves, but retracing the same period and ending at the same **end**. For example, chapter 6 (near the beginning of the prophetic section) ends with the great men of the earth calling for the *"rocks and the mountains to fall on them… for the great day of his wrath has come."* This is the **end**! But as we proceed we discover that earth's final history is being unfolded over again in chapters 13, 17, 18 and 19. As a matter of detail (as happens in Scripture regularly) the events of Chapter 17 seem to precede the events of Chapter 13. In the former, the ten horns are not crowned; in the latter, they are. When we return to Chapters 18 &19 we reach the **end** again, but from a different prospective, documenting the final end of Antichrist.

When studying Genesis 10 and 11, we saw that the interposition of the chapters meant the "system" produced the "man". The same is true in the visions of Revelation as we shall see. It is Babylon in mystery, that is about to be revealed, out of which Antichrist receives his power and eventually his domination of it.[2]

In chapter 17:4 *"a woman arrayed… decked with pearls."*

---

2   NOTE: it is not the purpose of these studies to give a commentary on Revelation, but to restrict ourselves to the references specifically relating to the final Apostasy.

Here we find Antichrist in the initial steps of his rise to power. Although he is seen as having **seven** heads and **ten** horns, they are uncrowned. He shares the glory of the woman and sustains her. He is coming from a position of obscurity to greatness. Regarding **Nimrod**: first, he is a servant to the **system** until he becomes strong enough to control it. In other words, the **system** produces the **man**, who will for a short time, dominate world affairs, first as its benefactor and then as its despot and head of a conspiracy against the Lord and His Anointed.[3]

The writer understands the **forth** empire of the great image in Daniel 2 to be the **Roman** empire, which will, at the time of the **last** apostasy, be restored in some form. Those who take this view generally accept it to be that area enclosed by the **great sea**, that is the Mediterranean Sea, in which **ten** geographical and political groupings (kingdoms) will emerge. Even if this is the case, there can be no doubt that the international community will be deeply affected by the activities of Antichrist and the eventual intervention of the Lord.

It might be helpful to list the main geographical areas that comprise the original Roman Empire:

1. In **Europe**: All the countries of Western and Southern Europe (excluding Ireland) including all the islands in the Mediterranean Sea, along with Turkey and ancient Dacia (Transylvania, Wallachia & Moldavia) now Romania and Moldova.

2. In **Asia**: The Euphrates was the south eastern limit, Arabia as the southern limit including Israel (the region now known as the Middle East).

3. In **Africa**: Egypt and the whole northern coast to Morocco.

---

3   NOTE: I digress here to explain the meaning of **world** in this context.

The Roman world *Orbis Terranum*, depository of the world's riches, is the main theatre of Antichrist's operations. We shall gradually see these countries brought into closer association. The distinction between the Greek and Latin divisions of the Roman Empire (the two legs of iron of Daniel's image) is still visible in its religious composition of Roman (West) and Orthodox (East) churches.

All will assume a system represented by the harlot of Chapter 17. By this time, as we have alluded to, these many countries will have been divided into the ten kingdoms referred to in Revelation. Although the exact geographical areas are unknown, it would seem more realistic that they will be controlled and energised not from Rome (Vatican City) but from a revived city of Babylon. Ecclesiastically, the Roman Catholic Church will play a very significant role, but it will be secondary to the economic regime controlled from Babylon.

"Seven mountains" (v. 9).

Many Bible scholars relate the seven mountains to Rome (sometimes called the "city of the seven hills") and conclude that Antichrist will be the product of the Roman Catholic system (the Harlot). As further proof of this they advance the persecutions referred to in verse 6, *"drunk with the blood of the saints,"* as those perpetrated by the Roman Catholic church down the centuries.

But on a closer examination, the evidence doesn't fit the facts: the whole Roman world is in view. Religious Rome has never controlled all the lands outlined above. Note that more than 50% (and rising) is under Islamic control.

Antichrist represents a secular position (included is the religious factor, but not exclusively as the Roman Church is).

Antichrist is depicted as a leopard (13:2); Rome is never depicted in this way.

Antichrist has an aide, the False Prophet. If as it is suggested, a Roman Pontiff is the Antichrist, who in the Roman system could this be?

Persecution cannot be restricted to the Roman church, it is

certainly included, but there is a much wider sphere of persecution. All **anti** Christian (the true Church of Jesus Christ) persecution is involved, but in an ever increasing way, Islam is the predominant persecutor. In the stages leading up to the end times, all the persecutors will unite, first of all against Israel (as detailed in Matthew 24 and Luke 21) and ultimately against the Lord and His Anointed (Psalm 2). It must also be pointed out that Orthodox Judaism is a fierce persecutor of Messianic believers. In Western Europe also (including the United Kingdom) it will soon be universally an offence to say that Jesus is the only way to Heaven (John 14:6; Acts 4:12).

We now return to Revelation 17:5, *"upon her forehead Mystery Babylon… I will tell the mystery of the woman."*

The *"mystery"* element is its hidden nature now about to be revealed. (In the New Testament a mystery is something that exists in the mind and purposes of God but we must wait for its revealing. The church of God, containing both Gentile and Jew, is an example Ephesians 3:3). Here, to use Zechariah's language, it appears out of the middle of the ephah, and becomes fully developed in a short period of time.

So to summarize, we can say that the stages of development are:

1. Its secret working in society from the Apostle Paul's day (2 Thess. 2).

2. It becomes connected to the ephah hidden, but soon to be revealed as lawlessness (Zech. 5).

3. It ceases to be hidden and is openly developed (Rev. 13; 17; 18).

"Drunken with the blood of the saints and with the martyrs of Jesus" (v. 6).

The system will become a fierce persecutor before it runs its course.

"The beast which you saw was and is not..." (v. 8).

This, in summary, describes the rise and fall of Antichrist

discussed when we consider chapters 13 and 19:18-21.

"And these are seven kings; five are fallen, the one is, and the other is not yet come..." (v. 10).

The most generally accepted interpretation of this is:

The five fallen are: Egypt, Assyria, Babylon, Media/Persia (the later being dominant) and Greece.

The one refers to Roman (the 4th Kingdom of the great Image, Daniel 2) which was still very much in power at the time of the Apostle John's writing, (exiled as he was by the Roman Emperor to Patmos for his faith in Jesus as Lord).

*"The **other** has not yet come."* Through the succeeding centuries governments reflected the iron/clay characteristics, that is strength/weakness culminating in the 20th /21st, centuries with democracies and presidential governments.

"The beast is an 8th and comes out of the 7th" (v. 11).

(Another evidence that the system produces the man.) Antichrist will be the last of earth's great rulers. That which was prophesied in the First Apostasy has now come to pass in the Last Apostasy.

We will revert to chapter 13 which comes next chronologically .

The Manifestation
Of Antichrist

The system is no longer predominant in this chapter for we have progressed now to **full** manifestation of the **beast** (Antichrist). The chapter too, introduces us to Antichrist's aide, the **false prophet**. We must not overlook the third and controlling personage of this evil trinity, the **dragon**, Satan, the instigator and manipulator of the whole apostasy against God, Christ and His saints.

In chapter 12 Satan, thrown down from heaven, has been actively engaged in Jerusalem and Israel. He now goes down to the **Great Sea** (Mediterranean) and calls up the one whom he is about to make lord of East and West.

Other monarchs have been Satan's servants, but Antichrist will be, in a special sense, his delegate. The False Prophet, the beast rising out of the earth (v. 11; commentators suggest that the "earth" here refers to the land of Israel, based on Matt. 24; Luke 21) represents the power of the ecclesiastical system that will develop and work in association with the secular power, but subservient to it.

"And he [the Dragon] *stood on the sand of the sea, I saw a beast coming up out of the sea"* (v. 1).

This infers that the dragon is looking Westward.

"Body of a leopard, feet like a bear, mouth like a lion" (v. 2). Compare this with Daniel 7:1-8, the same Beast is envisaged.

"Wounded as though it had been smitten to death" (v. 3). All who would behold this event would conclude that he was dead. *"As it were healed"* — this was a pseudo-resurrection which had two effects: the first to *"wonder,"* which led to *"worship."*

This worship is Satanically inspired (v. 4). This one is now no longer an ordinary man. He is transformed from the natural to the supernatural — a devil incarnate.

This Is The Final Apostasy

There are three Scriptural references to this:

2 Thessalonians 2:4, where he sets himself up in the temple as an object of worship.

Matthew 24:15, here he is referred to as standing in the "holy place" a direct reference to the inner sanctuary.

Daniel 9:27, the one who causes desolation is connected with the temple.

Since there is no temple in existence now, scripture is directing us to a building of the future, a temple again in Jerusalem, and to a sacrificial system, not as the Old Covenant, but as a commemoration of the death and resurrection of the Lord Jesus (Israel's Messiah) *and on his head the names of blasphemy."* This is now the full manifestation of the **lawless one**, and the iniquity that was hidden is now fully exposed (Zech 5; 2 Thess 2). In that day, society will be so depraved as to willingly accept blasphemy as normal.

"And there was given unto him a mouth speaking, great and blasphemous things" (v. 5). Compare:

Daniel 7:8	Rev. 13:8	A mouth speaking great things.
Daniel 7:21	Rev. 13:7	Made war with the saints.
Daniel 7:25	Rev. 13:5	A time, times and half a time that is, the last half of the tribulation period.

"His tabernacle" (v. 6). A reference to the existence of a temple in Jerusalem. (Psalm 2; 2 Thess. 2)[4]

"His tabernacle" (John 1:14; Rev. 21:3).

These represent two of the highest themes that belong to the majesty of God. If ever Satan overstepped the mark it is here.

---

4   NOTE: *"His Name"* cf John 17:6.

"War with make the saints" (v. 7). These saints are Jews and perhaps a wider people brought to faith in these terrible days, those referred to as not *"worshipping the image of the beast." "And to overcome them."* Even in this titanic struggle the people of God will not be immune from this calamity. *"Power* [authority] *given over every people and tongue and nation."*

Note the international flavour of this statement. These last day will mark a worldwide fixation with all that is happening in the Middle East and even into heavenly realms.

He was *"given"* authority. This is repeated twice. However Antichrist tries to win the primacy, he is not all-powerful and even the limited authority that he is given is for a limited time. His time is short. God, Jehovah, is in control of all, and His purposes will be fulfilled.

"All the inhabitants of the earth shall worship the beast, whose names have not been written in the Lambs book of life" (v. 8).

Again there is emphasis on world-wide involvement, and it is also a restatement that there will be very many (in the international context) who have heard the gospel and have trusted the Lord who will suffer for it. We need to note that there is only **one** Lamb's book of life, for every generation of mankind (Rev. 20:15).

Here is the *"patience and faith of the saints"* (v. 10). This verse is often used as a proof that the church will still be on the earth during the three and a half years of tribulation. Equally well it could apply to converts after the rapture of the church.

"And I saw another beast coming up out of the earth" (v. 11).

This introduces the False Prophet, the third member of the trinity of evil (v. 12).

Reference to the *"earth"* again refers to the prophetic earth. Many students believe this is a direct reference to Israel and that this 'man' will be a Jew.

*"Made the earth and inhabitants **worship** the beast* [ANTICHRIST]*"* (v. 12).

His role is more ecclesiastical than commercial. His first act is to inspire worship, followed by malicious signs.

"Fire from heaven" (v. 13-14).

A reenactment of Elijah's experience at Mount Carmel (2 Kings 18:38).

"Ordered them to set up an image....cause all who refused to worship the image of the beast to be killed" (v. 15).

To give breath to the image of the beast is obviously the very high point in the deceptive work of Antichrist. "Breath" translated *pneuma* is better translated spirit, that is an evil spirit in the image.

Men must either worship the beast or die!

The reference to *"as many"* widens the scale of the war being already waged against the saints. The flight of Israel (12:14), the persecution of the remnant and her seed (12:17) and the war with the saints (v.7) seems now to be carried world-wide against all who will not bow in worship to this evil speaking image.

These are the terrible days of which the Lord spoke (Matthew 24:22) *"except these days be shortened there should **no** flesh be saved."* The murder campaign of the **beast** will lead to genocide on an unprecedented scale. Jesus uses the words *"cut short"* to mean to *"terminate"* at the end of the 1260 day period.

The marvellous truth is that they will end by His return in awesome majesty and judgement on the Evil Trinity and on those that *"know not God or obey not the gospel of our Lord Jesus Christ"* (1 Thess. 1:7-9).

"To receive a mark on his right hand or forehead, so that no one could buy or sell, unless he had the mark, which is the name of the beast, or the number of the name. His number is 666" (v. 16).

This mark has its background in an old custom (see Isa. 44:5) or in the New Testament (Gal. 6:17), both indicating ownership. The worship of the beast and his claim to ownership crosses all the boundary lines of society.

"Buy or sell." An economic boycott. This is the final stage and speaks of a simple world-wide system of authorisation to purchase. The international use of code numbers to get access

to cash, to pay bills etc. is leading rapidly to a cashless society.

All transactions for each individual will demand a personal identification number. Experiments are currently underway relating to laser marking of the body. Instead of scanning a card, they scan the hand or the forehead — a frightening development.

In relation to the number 666 there have been numerous suggestions as to the meaning of this number. All of them are speculation and without an authoritative basis. Perhaps the nearest we can get is to suggest that '6' is the number of man. It just falls short of '7,' the number of perfection

Jesus, in Matthew 24 (already referred to) speaks of these horrific times and continues by referring to supernatural events.

"Immediately after those days" (v. 29-30) that is the darkness of the Great Tribulation sorrows

"sun darkened"

"moon not give its light"

"stars fall from heaven"

"sign of the Son of Man will appear in the sky"

"all nations of the earth shall mourn"

Luke 21:10 *"earthquakes, famines, pestilence, fearful events , great signs from heaven.*

A summary of events leading up to the end time (v. 12-19).

"When Jerusalem surrounded" (v. 20-24).

This is the end of all that a revived Roman Empire stands for. Note the concentration of military might against Jerusalem (cf Zech. 14).

Verses 25 and 26 reiterates what Matthew has said.

"At that time they shall see the Son of Man, coming in a cloud with great glory" (v. 27).

This summarized event is in two stages: there is the physical amassing of Gentile forces at Jerusalem and the terrible events that result from the invasion (Zech. 14:2).

There is the supernatural nature of the conflict. *"The Lord will go out and fight against those nations... the mount of Olives will split in two from East to West... and the Lord God shall come with all His holy ones with Him."*

The whole topographical features of Israel and the Middle East will be altered. Since the Flood nothing like it will have happened anywhere on the earth.

Returning again to Zechariah 14.

"Waters will flow out from Jerusalem..." (v. 8).

This is a great waterway from the Mediterranean, through Jerusalem to the Dead Sea, which will come alive again. The events described here and to the end of the chapter are taken generally to refer to the Millennial Kingdom.

Before that reign commences, there will be the final outpouring of God's wrath upon the evil trinity and the godless ones that follow them.

"Then were gathered together the kings to the place that is called Armageddon" (Rev. 16:16).

There appears, in these final days, to be two gatherings; one against Babylon with the invasion from the East and the drying up of the Euphrates and her final destruction as foretold in Isaiah 13, which includes both natural and supernatural events, where it refers to *"the stars and their constellations shall not show their light, the sun will be darkened and the moon will withhold its light...."*

Running parallel to this is the other great gathering of the armies at Armageddon. Reference is often made to the *'Battle of Armageddon"* but the word 'battle' does not appear in Scripture. There is no written evidence that there will be a battle there. It is a place of **gathering,** not **conflict**. The conflict, as we have seen will take place in the valley of Jehoshaphat outside Jerusalem, (Joel 3:2). *"I will gather all nations and bring them down to the valley of Jehoshaphat, there I will enter into judgement against them, concerning my inheritance and my people Israel...."* There the winepress is trodden. For them the day of the Lord has arrived as they are surrounding Jerusalem (Joel chapters 2 and 3).

Revelation 18 goes into extreme detail of the effect the fall of Babylon will have on its citizens and all who look to and trade in it.

However it is worth pointing out that five times in this chapter the term *"that great city"* (vv. 15-16, 18-19, 21) is mentioned and three times is added *"in one hour made desolate"* (vv. 15, 17, 19). These references add weight to the contention that this is a **literal** city and that its destruction is yet **future**.

Rev. 19:19. *"Then I saw the Beast and the kings of the earth and their armies gathered together to make war against the rider and his horse…"* (vv. 11-17). The Beast is captured and with him the False Prophet. The two of them are thrown into the Lake of Fire and the rest killed with the sword.

This is the **end** of the **last great apostasy**. The graphic account of Scripture in these closing chapters is beyond our full understanding and comment. We can but marvel at the majesty and awful might of the *"**Lord and His Anointed**"* (Ps. 2).

But for the redeemed of the Lord, it is only the beginning of unparalleled glory and the ushering in of the new creation (Rev. 21:1-6).

The Search For Answers

"And I applied my heart to know wisdom and to know madness and folly: I perceived that this was also a striving after wind. For in much wisdom is much grief, and he that increaseth knowledge increaseth sorrow" (Eccl. 1:17, 18).

We are told that we live in a post modern society—a society with no real answers, only questions and even the questions are questioned! The Modernist views the world as a community bound together in a common search for answers. Post modernism is a world of individuals in a sea of uncertainty. There are **no** absolutes anymore.

Someone said, "The world is no longer a scene, a place where the play is staged and directed towards a designed end. Instead it is obscene—a lot of noise and frantic activity without a plot." It leads to chaos, born out of pessimism and maintained by confusion.

Those of us who were brought up in the early and mid 20th century, experienced certainty and authority leading to a sense of security that will help us to see this post modern society for what it is. But, sadly, this is not the case with today's teenagers who have never known certainty. They will argue that there is no point in seeking after truth if there is no truth to be found; point in standing for what is right if there is nothing to measure it by. As the saying goes, "It is your right to believe what you want so long as you afford me the same right to believe something else."

Criticism has degenerated into cynicism. Everybody is encouraged to question everything, but no one, it seems, has the right to be definite about anything!

How different the situation is when we have the faith (God-given) to accept the veracity of God's word, and are able to say, "I know and am sure." Let us hold fast to the things which we have embraced and seek more earnestly the salvation of those beguiled by Satan's lies.

The Seven Great Words Of Galatians

(REFERENCES FROM THE REVISED VERSION)

1. **Revelation**: 1:12, 16; 2:2
2. **Liberation:** 2:4; 5:1-13
3. **Justification:** 2:16
4. **Crucifixion:** 2.20; 5.24; 6.14
5. **Unification:** 3:28
6. **Transformation:** 4:19
7. **Identification:** 6:17

The Apostle Paul travelled though Galatia on his second missionary journey, recorded in Acts 16:6, and again on his third journey three years later (Acts 18:23). He refers to his first preaching the Gospel with them when he wrote subsequent to those visits. It seems that on his second journey something quite alarming happened to his facial appearance, possibly to do with his eyes. It obviously caused him great concern and he was thankful that the new converts did not despise or reject him because of it (Gal. 4:12-15). There is a practical lesson here. It is that God can overrule in blessing despite seeming setbacks! It is also evident that he detected a change in atmosphere and beliefs among the saints (ch. 1:7). He refers to the preaching of *"another* [different] *gospel"*, to perverting or twisting around the gospel of Christ. In chapter 3:3 he speaks of *"works of the spirit done in the flesh."* He is concerned about their emphasis on the law, the observance of *"days, months, seasons and years,"* (ch. 4:10), and in chapter 5:2 their reliance on circumcision. All of this he summarises in his comment, *"O foolish Galatians, who did bewitch you before whose eyes Jesus Christ was openly set forth"* (3:1). The apostle, therefore, sets out to correct this deviation from the true gospel by establishing his apostolic authority. This takes up practically the whole of the introduction to his letter.

The key word to this introduction is **Revelation**. He refers to it in chapter 1:12, 16 and 2:2. In the three accounts of his conversion in the Acts there is no suggestion of his receiving any instructions about the gospel from Ananias. Verse 12 states quite clearly that he did not receive any details of the gospel *"from men".* In Ephesians 3:3-6 he speaks of *"the mystery of Christ given by revelation."* The word *"revelation"* is translated from *apokalupsis* which means to unveil or uncover; (*apo* from *halup* to uncover- the use here is objective and refers to something presented to the senses, sight or hearing. W.E. Vine). If we understand by the gospel, as preached by the apostle, the death, burial and resurrection of Christ, this he received by revelation. *"I received of the Lord that which also I delivered unto you."* In 1 Corinthians 15:3-4 when he wrote to the Roman believers he used the same word; *"I am not ashamed of the gospel... for therein is revealed the righteousness of God by faith"* (1:16-17). In Ephesians 3:3-5, he states the same truth *"...you have heard ...of the grace of God which was given me to you; how that by revelation was made known unto me the mystery... the mystery of Christ."* The Apostle Paul therefore stands uniquely apart from the other inspired writers in this underscoring of direct revelation from God. We know, too, of his account of the "in or out" of his body experience in 2 Corinthians 12:1-7 which may or may not be directly connected to these references in Galatians. It was upon this solid and incontrovertible foundation that he challenges and sets in order the errors they had espoused.

On a practical level there is an interesting reference to "revelation" in Philippians 3:14-16. *"I press toward the goal of the upward calling of God in Christ Jesus. Let us therefore , as many as be perfect* [mature], *be thus minded, and if in anything ye are otherwise minded, even this God shall reveal it unto you."* Believers are to pursue the same objective as the apostle, that is, to look forward and not back. If they were tempted to dwell on a lower level and to desist from pressing forward to the goal, God would reveal the truth to them even if eventually it meant chastening. This seems to be the import of Hebrews 12:5-11, where the goal is to be *"partakers of His holiness."* The method of this revelation will not come through visions and dreams but by the Holy Spirit's intervention through the Word of God.

The second great word is embodied in the truth of **Liberation**. In chapter 2:4 he talks about *"our liberty in Christ."* He continues the theme in chapter 5, which commences with the word *"freedom"* defending it in a most robust way. *"Stand fast therefore, and be not entangled again in a yoke of bondage." "You were running well; who did hinder you that you should not obey the truth"* and *" he that troubleth you all bear his judgement, whosoever he be"* (vv. 1, 7 and 10).The first three verses of this chapter are in one sense the key to understanding the main message of his letter. In a nut shell, it is not a matter of ritual but of faith — faith in the Son of God and their incorporation into Him, through His death, burial and resurrection. This is the basis of the new Covenant and there could be no thought of reverting to the rites and restrictions of the Old one. Hebrew 1:1-6 teaches that *"Christ as a Son over His own house"* is superior to *"Moses as a servant over his house."* And so in chapter 2:13 there is the call to "liberty", to serve God, not according to the letter of the law, but in the energy and fullness of the Spirit. We remind ourselves of the injunction of the apostle to the Roman believers, *"But now, we have been discharged from the law, having died to that wherein we were holden, so that we serve the newness of the spirit and not in the oldness of the letter"* (Rom. 7:6).

Our third word is **Justification**. The great truth the apostle propounds here he enlarges on when he come to write the letter to the Christians in Rome. *"Yet knowing that a man is not justified by the works of the law but through faith in Jesus Christ, even we have believed in Jesus Christ, that we might be justified by faith in Christ, and not by works of the law: for by the law shall no flesh be justified"* (ch. 2:16).

Justification is an objective truth. It originates in God, and rests on His immutability and unchanging character. It is the act of God in removing from the believing sinner the penalty of death due to his sin and imparting to him the righteousness of His Son.

In other words, God sees us perfect and complete in Christ. Twice over, in Acts 22:14 and 1 John 2:1, the Lord Jesus is called the *"Righteous One"* and the apostle Paul tells the Corinthian believers that *"Christ Jesus was made unto us wisdom from God and Righteousness…"* (1 Cor. 1:30). The truth of the matter is that God in Christ has forgiven all, has cancelled all and has forgotten all! This is the ground of the believer's triumph. The saving work of Christ closes every mouth, dismisses every accusation and ignores every threat that can be brought against us. There is no other standard by which saved sinners can stand before Him. It is not in any sense *"of works lest any man should boast"*. The performing of good works results from the workmanship of God in the believer's life (Eph. 2:9-10).

The fourth word is **Crucifixion**. *"I have been crucified with Christ…"* (ch. 2:20). What a statement! What did He mean? In Romans 6:8 he says, *"If we died with Christ, we believe that we shall also live with him."* The tenses indicate something that happened in the past and would be completed in the future. But how far back do we go? Some go back to a baptism that they say makes them inheritors of the Kingdom of God, but that surely contradicts the teaching of this epistle. Some believe that it happened at the moment of conversion when eternal life was imparted. I think, however, that the apostle went farther back—back to Calvary! When the Lord Jesus cried, *"It is finished,"* He meant this in the fullest possible sense. It encompassed all those who had and would trust Him by faith. He looked backward and forward down the ages and saw it all accomplished. He called it His baptism (Luke 12:50). And in that baptism all believers are included. To personalise it: when He died, I died in Him; when He was buried I was buried in Him and when he was resurrected, so was I! If this is so, it means that when I trusted Christ and commenced to walk in *"newness of life"* (Rom. 6:4), I came into the good of all that He accomplished in His death, burial and resurrection. My baptism by immersion in water was my public identification with Christ in His baptism and an act of obedience to Him as He had commanded. Finally, the apostle sees this crucifixion as having important on-going implications. In chapter 6:14 he sees not one but three crucifixions: his Lord's, his own and the world's. What a challenge to us who are united to Christ.

Word number five is **Unification**. *"Ye are all one* [man] *in Christ Jesus"* (ch. 3:28). Jew, Gentile, bond, free, male and female are listed. This does not do away with nationality or gender. Rather it puts all categories of believers on the same basis and on the same level – equally one in Christ. This is an indissoluble union; it can never be ruptured or annulled. The hymn writer has caught the true meaning: *"Once in Christ, in Christ for ever, thus the eternal covenant stands."*

In John 10:27-28, the good Shepherd announces the terms of being one of His sheep. *"I give unto them eternal life and they shall never perish, neither shall any man pluck them out of My Father's hand. I and My Father are one."* The uniqueness of this unity He expresses and emphasises further to His disciples, *"If any man love Me he will keep My word: and My Father will love him and We will come unto him and make our make our abode with him"* (John 14:23). The same apostle, in the introduction to his first letter, links this to the idea of fellowship, partnership or communion: *"That which we have seen and heard, declare we unto you also, that ye also may have fellowship with us; yea and our fellowship is with the Father and with His Son Jesus Christ"* (1 John 1:3). As we listen to the very heart throb of the Son to the Father in His intercessory prayer, we realize what the continuing unity of His own meant to Him. While they could never be separated as to their position in Him, there could be a disruption in fellowship and that could benefit only *"the evil one."* Hence the prayer's intensity: *"Holy Father, keep them in thy name, which thou hast given me, that they may be one even as we are"* (John 17:11).

Our penultimate word is **Transformation**. *"My little children, of whom I travail in birth again until Christ be formed in you"* (ch. 4:19). This is the high-water mark of Christian living. It is a blessed fact to be **in** Christ, but to have Christ **formed** in us is quite another matter. W.E.Vine in his *Dictionary Of New Testament Words* explains: "This refers not to the external and transient, but to the inward and real… It expresses the necessity of a change in character and conduct to correspond with inward spiritual condition, so that there may be moral conformity to Christ." It is important to note the word **until**. The apostle does not say "might". He is confident that this transformation can take place, but at the cost of his continued intervention and intercession in spiritual birth pains. It entails anxiety, labour and wrestling in prayer for them. This begs the question, who is doing this for **us** now?

Many of us have had as spiritual mentors those who have *"watched for our souls"* (Heb. 13:17). Perhaps this goes some way in finding an answer. But we know, too that *"the Spirit Himself maketh intercession for the saints according to the will of God"* (Rom. 6:23-27).

Our final great word is **Identification**. *"I bear branded on my body the marks of Jesus"* (ch. 6:17). It seems best to take this text literally and see these as physical scars, the evidence of vicious thrashings at the hands of the enemies of his Lord. Acts 16:23 refers to *"many stripes,"* 2 Corinthians 6:5 *"in stripes"* and chapter 11:25, *"thrice was I beaten with rods"*. As in this first century, so the persecution of those who identify themselves as believers in the One true God and His Son Jesus Christ continues with unrelenting fury. This is an area of Christian profession that we who live in freedom should feel very uncomfortable with. 2 Timothy 2:12, tells us plainly that *"if we suffer [endure] with Him we shall also reign with Him: if we shall deny Him, He also will deny us."* I often ask myself, Is God partial? In other words, Why have some places in our world, notably in what we call "the West," been spared physical and psychological persecutions while for millions of other believers in many lands it has been and is still their common lot? If we consider carefully and prayerfully the present condition of our so-called free world we can only conclude that there are dark clouds on the horizon. Restrictions on Christian teaching and testimony are now gaining a frightening momentum. The intensity of evil and sheer Godlessness is bound soon to reap a harvest of judgement. A correct reference is often made to the imminent return of the Lord Jesus for His Church. Is it possible that before He gives the "shout" we too here in free and favoured countries may have to face an onslaught of suffering shame for His name? Something I think we should ponder!

The Shepherd Sin-Bearer

"Who his own self bare our sins in his own body on the tree that we, having died unto sins, might live unto righteousness: by whose stripes ye were healed. For ye were going astray like sheep; but are now returned unto the Shepherd and Bishop of your souls" (1 Pet. 2:24).

As Shepherd He would lead and as Bishop (Overseer/Pastor) He would provide. But who are these sheep? They are those His Father had given Him. *"My Father which hath given them unto, me, is greater than all; and no one is able to snatch them out of the Father's hand"* (John 10:29). This is but one reference from those mentioned in the Shepherd discourse in this chapter and in His High Priestly prayer in chapter 17. The sad fact is, however, that the sheep were lost and had to be rescued. They were spiritually dead in trespasses and sins and the Good Shepherd came to seek and to save them. The Apostle Peter now details for us the nature and cost to the Shepherd of that rescue.

"Who His own self":

This speaks of **Sovereignty**. At His birth the angel declared to the shepherds, *"...there is born to you this day in the city of David a Saviour which is Christ the Lord"* (Luke 2:11). There was no other suited to be a Saviour. *"He only,"* as Frances Alexander puts it, *"could unlock the gates of heaven and let us in."* No lesser person could measure up to this great work. Human sin could be dealt with only by One who was SINLESS! So the apostle gives primacy of place to the method of putting away sin.

"bare our sins":

This introduces us to the truth of **substitution**. This word in the Old Testament speaks of the priest carrying the sacrifice up to the brazen altar. Alford says; "this word belongs to sacrifice and should not be disassociated from it." The prophet Isaiah states in anticipation of that sacrifice; *"...the Lord hath laid (made to meet) on him the iniquity of us all"* (Isaiah 53:6). He had to bare them before He could take them away. His death was adequate to deal with the sin of the world. That was the cry of the Baptist at the Jordan, *"Behold the Lamb of God; which taketh away the sin of* *the world"* (John 1:29). The just gave Himself for the unjust, the sinless for the sinful; He gave His riches for our poverty, His death for our life.

"in His own body":

Sacrifice: own self! **Own** body! The emphasis must not be overlooked: self, that is the person; body, that is the vehicle that housed the person. Truly Man yet truly God! This brings us to consider the nature and character of His death. The use of **"in"** instead of **"on"** signifies more than physical suffering. That body contained a soul and a spirit. The soul, His life and emotions felt the pain to the depth of His innermost being. Psalm 22 prophetically captures that intensity; *"...I sink in the deep mire where there is no standing, all thy waves and billows have gone over me."* In relation to His spirit, that is where we withdraw from human comment. As already quoted from Isaiah: *"God made to meet on Him the iniquity of us all."* It was in His spirit that He became answerable for the sin of the world. Abandoned and forsaken! Small wonder the sun refused to shine! This is where a full atonement was transacted, where propitiation with His Father was accepted and where our redemption was accomplished resulting in the triumphant cry: *"It is finished."*

"on the tree":

What **Shame**! Kenneth Wuest speaking of this says, "The Greek word translated "tree," does not mean a literal tree but an object fashioned out of wood. In this case a Cross." On it He, the spotless Lamb of God, was suspended between heaven and earth, as if fit for neither. It was the greatest insult and curse that could be heaped upon any convict and common criminal yet He, untarnished and unsullied, willingly accepted the indignity and shame so that we, poor wretched vile sinners, could be lifted to the heights of heavenly glory!

"that we being dead to sin should live unto righteousness":

Sanctification: dead to sins, that is, set apart, speaks of God's action in love and grace in breaking the control and power of the sin nature in the believer's life. This is the great argument discussed by the Apostle Paul in Romans 6:

Verse 6   *"…no longer in bondage to sin,"*

Verse 11   *"…reckon yourselves dead unto sin,"*

Verse 12   *"…let not sin reign in your mortal body that you should obey the lusts thereof."*

Verse 13   *"…neither present your members unto sin as instruments of unrighteousness: but present yourselves to God, as alive from the dead, and your bodies as instruments of righteousness, by whose stripes we are healed."*

The Greek word translated "stripes" is singular, not plural.

Kenneth Wuest comments: "Peter remembered the scourging of his Lord, His flesh so badly mangled that the disfigured form appeared to his eyes as one single bruise."

The physical sufferings, the depths of man's iniquity and the spiritual sufferings, the extent of God's love are inextricably bound together in this act of salvation.

The Trystings Of Love

"With desire I have desired to eat this Passover with you before I suffer... and he took bread and when he had given thanks, he brake it, and gave it to them saying, 'This is My body which is given for you this do in remembrance of Me.' And the cup in like manner after supper [the Passover], *saying, 'This cup is the new covenant* [agreement] *in My blood, even that which is poured out for you'"* (Luke 22:15-20 RV).

This Passover would be different from all the previous celebrations in the Lord's short life. From the age of twelve He would have been able, in His home in Nazareth, to partake of this annual feast. In the three years of His public ministry He probably celebrated it with His disciples and close friends. This one, however, was different and very special. When the official Passover meal was concluded their Master reached again for the bread and breaking it said, *"My body — given for you."* He passed it around and they all partook for the second time. What would their thoughts have been? I think I can see the confused looks on many faces! But the drama continued and intensified, He reached forward again and took one of the Passover cups and called it the *"new covenant in **My** blood which is poured out for you."*

How strange! A **new** covenant in **My** blood!!

It is true that their history was steeped in covenants and covenant making. Indeed it had also been a history of covenant breaking! And they were very familiar with blood covenants. But to try to comprehend what a covenant in their Master's blood could possibly mean was enough to unhinge their minds. Not only was it new because of this, but also because it would be a covenant, not between two parties but **one** party. God would covenant with Himself, in His Son. Divinity would make an agreement with Divinity. That would make it permanent and forever secure. It could never be broken. This is the story explained in great detail in the Hebrews letter.

This covenant when enacted would affect all it embraced in a number of ways. And, it would take the disciples a lifetime to understand the far reaching implications of it, as direct revelations and the Holy Spirit would enlighten them.

1. It would affect their **religious** life.

As sons of Israel they were the possessors of the only God-given religion. Through sacrifice, Tabernacle and Temple, God had given them a special privilege of fellowship and worship. They were **near** to God, not like the Gentiles (nations) around them who were *"without God and without hope"* (Eph. 2:12). They, in contrast, were loved with an *"everlasting love"* (Deut. 28:9) *"… that He may establish thee as a holy people unto Himself that He may be unto thee God."*

Now this **new** covenant would change all that, and in the immortal words of the Good Shepherd, this covenant would bring in *"other sheep not of this* [Jewish] *fold!"* (John 10:16).

This was like standing all these disciple knew and revered upon its head! Peter's experience on the housetop with the sheet and animals, clean and unclean, in itself illustrates how difficult the whole concept was (Acts 10). Added to this there was his retreat from eating with Gentile believers in Antioch when visited there by James and suffering a stinging rebuke from his fellow apostle, Paul (Gal. 2:12-19).

Praise God the vast majority of us are the "other" sheep!

2. Then it would affect them **politically**.

They had been taught that there was coming a **Messiah** a conquering King, who would deliver them from all their woes, sorrows and afflictions. He was prophesied to rule from *"shore to shore"* (Ps. 72). He would drive out the invaders for good, and give them peace. While in the calendar of God all this would ultimately come to pass, the new covenant would proclaim that, before there could be national salvation, there would have to be individual salvation, by the remission of sins, through the blood of His cross! This unfolding message led to more problems for them as hinted at in the disciples' question after the Resurrection. *"Wilt Thou **at this time** restore the kingdom to Israel?"*(Acts 1:6).

They might also have recalled one of their Master's answer to Pilate, *"My kingdom is not of this world."* The laws of the **new** Covenant would be written, not on parchment or stone, but on their hearts and that would lead all who would embrace this covenant as a priority to consider that they were citizens of a *"heavenly country"* (Heb. 11:16).

3. Finally it would affect them **economically**.

Under the previous or Old Covenant the nation of Israel was promised a land that would be especially blessed materially (Deut. 28:2-8). Blessings and prosperity would however, depend on **obedience**. But under the New Covenant obedience would not automatically be followed by material prosperity.

One of those who reclined at the table with him was Peter, the apostle who years later addressed his letter to the *"elect who are sojourners of the dispersion"* (1 Pet. 1). In modern language they were 'refugees.' They had lost everything and were now seeking some kind of economic stability on foreign shores.

The Apostle Paul, too, reflects on the effect the New Covenant had on him, *"What things were gained to me, those I counted loss for Christ"* (Phil. 3:5-8). Perhaps the most stark statement characterising life under the New Covenant is found in 2 Timothy 3:12. *"They that will live godly in Christ Jesus, shall suffer persecution."* I find this a searching, even devastating, concept in the context of Western "Christian" values! However, we must remember that this truth was articulated to the disciples by their Lord, *"If any man would come after Me, let him deny himself and take up his cross and follow Me... for what is a man* [disciple] *profited if he gain the whole world and lose or forfeit his own self"* (Luke 9:23-26 R.V.).

The Virgin Birth

Non-belief in the virgin birth leaves us with serious conse-quences as to who Christ is. If his life, as recorded in the Gospels and referred to in the Epistles, is miraculous and His exit from death also miraculous, then belief in the virgin birth must be a reality. Sinlessness demands a miraculous origin.

"The angel answered and said unto her [Mary], *The Holy Ghost shall come upon thee and the power of the Most High shall overshadow thee; wherefore also that which is to be born shall be called holy, the son of God"* (Luke 1:35).

This conception by the Holy Spirit is only the beginning of a series of inexplicable human facts covering a period of thirty years.

At the dawn of human life and the tragic consequences of the fall of man came a remarkable prophetic statement by the Creator. *" I will put enmity between thee* [Satan] *and the woman* [Eve] *between thy seed and **her** seed…"* (Gen. 3:15). The normal course of generation is through the seed of the man, but it is quite clear from Matthew's account of the angels' visitation to Joseph that the conception of his betrothed had already taken place. He was in no way involved. Hence his devastation at the news that the one he loved and trusted was expecting a child! The angel in a dream told him—*" Joseph, thou son of David, fear not to take unto thee Mary thy wife, for that which **is** [already] con-ceived in her IS of the Holy Ghost"* (Matt. 1:20).

Furthermore the angel announced the child's name! *"And she shall bring forth a Son; and thou shall call His name **Jesus**…"* (Matt. 1:21). This is similar to the angel's declaration to Mary (Luke 1:31). So both were together to be responsible for nam-ing the child. In Matthew's account, however, there is a very important addition, *"…He shall save His people from their sins."*

As quoted above the angel used the word "holy" to char-acterise this child. No one before Him or since has been born "holy" and certainly no one ever born, apart from this One has been called "Son of God." That speaks of pre-existence. God is eternal; His Fatherhood is equally eternal. If there is an eternal Father, then the Son **must** be eternal. We must remember that the full mystery of this One was revealed neither prior to (by the Jewish prophets and now the angel), or at His birth. His Mother Mary was not given the full story. The whole truth, including pre-existence would be manifested in His life, work, claims, death, resurrection, ascension, present ministry and coming again, would be expanded upon and would corroborate His own statement, *"I came out* (from beside—equality of deity) *from the father, and am come into the world, again I leave the world and go unto the Father"* (John 16:28).

The oft-repeated and well-known trio of confirmation of the sinlessness of the Lord Jesus is reserved to His apostles: *"He **did** no sin..."* (1 Pet. 2:22). *"He **knew** no sin..."* (2 Cor. 5:21). *"**In Him** was no sin..."* (John 3:5). His very nature, mind-set and actions are untainted, untarnished and unspotted! Well might Pilate say, *"I find no fault in this man"*! Belief in the absolute perfection of this One and belief in His miraculous conception stand or fall together. To believe that in the smallest degree the "holiness" of Jesus was not an inseparable part of His nature would condemn Him as a sinner to need regeneration. In another context the apostle Paul's denial is none too strong, **God forbid**!

I close this brief and introductory study of a great and undeniable truth by quoting the late Professor James Orr: "A sinless man is as much a miracle in a moral world as the virgin birth is a miracle in the natural world."

"This" Rock

"When Jesus came into the coasts of Caesarea Philip, He asked His disciples, saying, 'Whom do men say that I the Son of man am?' And they said, 'Some say that Thou art John the Baptist; some Elias; and others Jeremias, or one of the prophets.' He saith unto them, 'But who say ye that I am?' And Simon Peter answering said, 'Thou art the Christ the Son of the living God.' And Jesus answered and said unto him, 'Blessed art thou Simon Barjona; for flesh and blood hath not revealed it unto thee, but My Father which is in heaven. And I say unto thee, Thou art Peter and upon this rock I will build My church; and the gates of hell shall not prevail against it'" (Matt. 16:13-18).

At first reading, it seems strange that the Lord took His disciples on a two day journey, to the most northern part of Israel at the border with Lebanon, to ask the question, Who do men say that I am? Could He not as easily have asked it in one of the local towns by the sea of Galilee? The question arose in the week before the Lord's death. For over three years He had proclaimed Himself the Son of God, only to be ridiculed and rejected.

The place, however, was highly significant. It was here that the children of Dan set up for themselves graven images making this location the cult centre for the northern tribes of Israel (Judg. 18:28-30). They called it Dan after the name of their father. Later it became corrupted to Pan, after the goat god, then became Panius. Because of pronunciation difficulties, it became Banias. The occupying power renamed it Caesarea Philippi after the Roman Emperor. To this day the place is dominated by a massive rock where niches cut out of the stone can be clearly seen, which once held the idols of Dan's day.

The disciples were challenged on the very spot that symbolised their forefather's rejection of the living God. The question really was, would they make the same mistake? Simon Peter's answer, "Thou art the Christ the Son of the living God," spoke for the disciples. The Lord then revealed the glorious truth that in contrast to Dan's rock, Peter's confession was **the** rock upon which He would build His church.

But what about the nation? Would they accept Him? Sadly not. In less than a week's time they gave their answer, *"We will not have this man to reign over us."*

How true the saying that "History has the habit of repeating itself!"

Unmerited Favour

I.

"Blessed be the God and Father of our Lord Jesus Christ, who hath blessed us with all spiritual blessings in heavenly places in Christ. According as He hath chosen us in Him, before the foundation of the world, that we should be holy and without blame before Him in love" (Eph. 1:3-4).

This introduction to Paul's letter to the Ephesian believers outlines the perfection and finality of the work of Christ—a work in which we had no part, assuring us of a salvation which is comprehensive and eternal.

The first **key** word used by the Apostle is **"chosen"** *"...even as He hath chosen us..."*. Who is **He**?—*"...the Father of our Lord Jesus Christ."* This speaks of Divine Sovereignty—God's prerogative to choose. He is the Potter, we are the clay. In His electing grace, I am happy now to say that He chose me!

God chose Israel, not for any special merit on their part. To effect that choice, He spoke to an idolater in Ur of the Chaldees, told him to leave home and travel westward to an unknown land, which He had selected. From this land God would multiply his seed *"as the stars of the heavens, and as the sands upon the sea shore"* (Gen. 22:17). From this one man came a nation, and out of that nation came the Messiah—Jesus the Saviour.

It was prophetically said of Him, *"He shall see his seed, He shall prolong his days and the pleasure of the Lord shall prosper in His hand"* (Isa. 53.10). Over the centuries, succeeding generations have marvelled at the fulfilment of this prophecy. However, it will not be until He calls His blood-washed, chosen possession to Himself in the coming day of His glory, that the seed of Abraham and of the woman will be finally revealed.

ALL of it, *"after the counsel of His own will!* (Ephesians 1.11)

II.

The remarkable thing about God's choice is that it happened before the foundation of the world!

God saw the Ephesian believers before the creation of mankind and marked them out for His salvation. Is this choice exclusive to the Ephesians? The apostle addresses his letter to *"the saints at Ephesus,"* but quickly adds, *"and to the faithful in Christ Jesus"* (v. 1). Chapter 6:24 also assures us that the letter was written to *"all who love our Lord Jesus Christ with an undying love."* Every believer has been chosen in Christ, from God's standpoint. This is important. Man had no part in this choice — he could not, for he had not yet been created.

Saul of Tarsus was not aware of his election when he went on his murderous escapade to Damascus, nor was he aware of the fact (as he revealed at a later date) that he had been *"separated from his mother's womb"* that God might *"reveal His Son in me, that I might preach Him among the heathen"* (Gal. 1:15-16). He just did not know that, when he set out to persecute the fledgling church, the very message which he despised and hated, he would one day proclaim *"to be the power of God unto salvation to every one that believes"* (Rom. 1:16).

We have been chosen; this is the declaration of the God who cannot lie. But we will not know this until we believe. Election is the **Gospel** for the believer! This involves faith in God, an implicit trust that His word is His bond.

Northern Ireland, my home country, is "big" on banners and arches! They depict heroic events political and religious, and are paraded in processions generally in the June-August period each year. They have highly colourful pictures painted on both sides. I sometimes think that this idea of a message on both sides illustrates the truth of election. God has an arch, it has writing on both sides; as a sinner I survey the first message *"Whosover believeth hath everlasting life."* I accept the message and pass underneath and look at the writing on the back side. It proclaims in unambiguous words, "Chosen in him from before the foundation of the world!"

We can join with Toplady's stanza:

Chosen not for good in me,
Wakened up from wrath to flee,
Hidden in the Saviour's side,
By the spirit sanctified.
What a revelation!

III.

"…that we should be holy and without blame before Him in love" (v. 4).

There are two further things that we must not miss here. There is an objectivity to this choosing. It is not a mindless transaction, without reason behind it.

We are chosen to be **holy**! And we are chosen to be **blameless**!

God is **holy**, that is one of His attributes. It is not just that He acts in a holy way, but He is holy in Himself. That is His nature. Hence the injunction written by the Apostle Peter; *"Be ye holy for I am holy"* (1 Pet. 1:16).

Holiness implies integrity, honesty and truth in the inward parts. God wants us to be like Himself so He regenerates us: *"… according to his mercy he saved us, by the washing of regeneration and renewing of the Holy Spirit; which he shed on us abundantly through Jesus Christ our Saviour"* (Tit. 3:5-6).

He does not ask us to be sinless. In this fallen world that is just not possible. But we are given a Divine life, a regenerated life and in it there is intrinsic power—power to resist, overcome and be victorious! We cannot take one step in holiness without this regeneration. It is one thing to be forgiven all our sins because of the sacrifice of Calvary; but unless we can now live as those worthy of the One who has forgiven us, our salvation is incomplete.

Thank God today for the washing of regeneration, a new birth from above! This is expressed in another way, by the apostle writing to the church at Corinth. He tells them that: *"If any man be in Christ, he* [there] *is a new creation, the old has passed away and the new has come"* (2 Cor. 5:17). The new creation is the living Lord within, in the person of the Holy Spirit, giving the authority and the power over sin, which still wants to reign. The apostle emphasises this again in his treatise in Romans (chapter 6:11-23). In summary he says, *"…reckon ye yourselves to be dead unto sins, but alive unto God in Christ Jesus, Let not sin reign in your mortal body, that ye should obey the lusts thereof… for sin shall not have dominion over you, ….and being made free from sin, ye became the servants of righteousness…."*

It is from this regenerated life that holiness issues.

Following the objective of holiness there is a significant phrase: "without blame." Not, "without fault," for that, like sinlessness, as we have seen, is an impossibility while we remain in these bodies. God will take into account our frail and failing humanity and its many faults, some of which cannot be defined as sin. We forget or overlook something, we are at fault, but what about being to blame?

Faultlessness has to do with my nature; blamelessness has to do with my motives! What really matters is how I think, what is behind my thinking, why I do what I do. Is my thinking good, is my motive pure? I may have been at fault in my method of communication, or mistaken in my action, but it was never my intention to wound or hurt. This is to be "without blame, before Him in love." Love is the lubricant, the atmosphere in which we act and interact. This allows us to be worthy of the One whom we serve and who called us out of darkness into His marvellous light.

Dr. Sidlow Baxter, when he was a little boy in a poor Yorkshire (England) home, watched his mother prepare to go to church. It was a very dark and cold night. As she dressed in the bedroom he noticed her shoes sitting nearby so he decided to warm them for her. He lifted them and put them into the oven—a space in the chimney breast—sealed off with an iron door. When his mother came seeking them and he told her what he had done, she retrieved ashes, not shoes!

Dr. Baxter comments simply, "I was not faultless, but I was blameless, for I loved my mother dearly."

The apostle, therefore, has no hesitation in exhorting his readers to be without blame.

IV.

"Having predestinated us unto the adoption of children by Jesus Christ to Himself, according to the good pleasure of His will. To the praise of the glory of His grace, wherein He hath made us accepted in the beloved" (vv. 5-6).

In the Divine mind the "choosing" and the "predestination" are one act, independent of time. Someone has said: "Election is choosing out a number, destined beforehand for a purpose." In this case, that purpose was that He could adopt us as children. This is the sovereign act of God.

In Roman law an adopted child had the right to the material possessions of the one adopting him. It also meant he had a civil status—a name, so that he could take his full place in the community.

Using this as an illustration, God takes me, a believing sinner—and regenerates me. With this new life He makes me His child, and gives me the legal position of one of His sons, one of those born into His family. This is the significance of the expression, *"We have been made joint heirs with Christ"* (Rom. 8:17) And marvel of marvels it is all done *"according to the good pleasure of His will."* God's emotions are towards me and, by His grace, in His own goodness, entirely of His own choosing, He makes me His child.

This is certainly unmerited favour. Like the apostle, we should be thrilled with a sense of praise and glory that will lead to kindness and love to those who are so unlovable.

The truth of Adoption, above other truths of Scripture affects me very deeply.

My late father was an evangelist and Bible teacher. On his travels he would be asked about his family. He would usually reply in the words of the parable, *"A certain man had two sons"* (Luke 15:1). I was the older of the two and, when I was seventeen, I became aware of a recurring conversation between my father and mother. It went something like this, "Wouldn't it be good to have a little girl in our home, the boys would enjoy having a little sister!"

We all agreed that we should put the plan into action, and in due course a little girl, a few months old arrived in our home. There was great rejoicing. However, this was tempered by the fact that a series of procedures had to be gone through before the adoption was legal. It was an anxious and uncertain time. Frequently the thought passed through our minds, and we even voiced it, "Could someone come and take her from us?" It was a marvellous day when all the legalities were completed. I can still recall lifting out that precious little gurgling bundle, holding her tight, and saying tearfully, "You are my own little sister, no one can take you from us now."

I learned, in a very practical way that once a child is in the family, he/she is a family member for good. No amount of failure can alter it.

Someone reading this today may be despairing as to whether you have been, or could ever be, fully forgiven, and if it was possible that you could cease to be a child of the Father. Let me remind you: Your relationship to your Father in heaven is *"according to the good pleasure of His will."* Though we do not now, or ever in the future, merit such a status, we have the *"right to be called the sons of God"* (1 John 3:1) and to enjoy all the rights and privileges of sonship.

V.

"In whom we have redemption through His blood, the forgiveness of sins, according to the riches of His grace" (v. 7).

We have been **chosen, predestinated** and **adopted** as sons of God. Now we are told we have been **redeemed**.

Why did the apostle use the word "redemption"? He was a Jew, and from his earliest days, he had been educated in the truth that atonement depended upon the sacrificial system as instituted in the Torah (the first five books of the Old Testament scripture, written by Moses). Now regenerated and taught by the Holy Spirit and by revelation, Paul centred all atonement in the one sacrifice of His Lord. He would have in mind the mercy seat, the propitiatory (the place of satisfaction), where the sprinkled blood spoke of guilt, confession and acceptance on the grounds of substitution. In the Levitical system, the blood of animals was substituted. In contrast to this, in the sacrifice of Christ, the Offerer became the Victim and gave Himself as a substitute for our sins (Heb. 9:26).

It is with this as his doctrine of the atonement, the apostle here introduces us to redemption. The comforting thing is that it is in the present tense—"....in whom we are having redemption." Redemption is a fact that abides from the past into the present and on to the future, as we shall shortly see.

For the believer, redemption is always undisturbed and undiluted by time. Whether today, or tomorrow, God will remain true to His word: "Your sins are forgiven for His name's sake" (1 John 2:12).

In the word "forgiven" is the idea of release—letting sins go, as though they had not been committed.

It is like setting a prisoner free or discharging a debt.

The consensus among Bible scholars will define "redemption" as releasing by the payment of a price. The price is technically described as "ransom money".

Kenneth Wuest says: The story of redemption can be told in three Greek words:

1. *agorazo* -to buy in the slave market (1 Cor. 6:20).

2. *exagorazo* -to buy out the slave market (Gal. 3:13).

3. *lutroo* -to liberate by payment of a ransom (Tit 2:14).

The good news, the Gospel is that the Lord Jesus Christ bought us in the slave market of sin. He paid the ransom price—His blood—to deliver us from the tyranny of sin and its master Satan, whose slaves we were (Rom. 6:17).

We learn from Leviticus 17:11 that *"the life of the flesh is in the blood."* The value in the blood of Christ lies in its ownership; it is the blood of God's beloved Son. This makes it "precious" blood (1 Pet. 1:19) which He poured out for us in His atoning death.

William Blane in his poem "The Atonement", says

"If all the sins of all the world,

In heaven's balances were laid,

They would be outweighed by Jesus' death."

The death of Christ, signified in the outpouring of His blood, satisfied the righteous demands of a just God and His holy law. In New Testament parlance God's law stated that *" the wages of sin is death, but the gift of God—the acceptance of the Lord's sacrifice on our behalf—is eternal life…"* (Rom. 6:23). Not only are we bought out of the slave market, but we are out for good! We will never be dominated by sin and Satan again. The Lord Jesus has bought us, not only to liberate us, but, as we have seen, to adopt us as His sons.

The idea of being out of the slave market for good is developed by the apostle in his Colossian letter, when he talks about *"being delivered from the authority of darkness and transferred into the kingdom of the Son of His love"* (Col. 1:13). The writer in Hebrews 9:26 also tells us that sin has been *"put away."* The underlying thought is "to send them away." This surely must be Calvary's message. Let hymnology come to aid our worshipping hearts:

An end of my sin has been made for me here,

By Him who its penalty bore,

With blood it is blotted eternally out,

And I will not remember it more.

HEART WARMING TRUTHS

I am reminded of the ceremony surrounding the two little animals on the Day of Atonement. One was killed and its blood placed before God in the inner tabernacle behind the veil. God was resident there in the cloud of glory—the Shekinah. The nation's sins were confessed over the other goat, then, symbolically laden with sins it was led away into the wilderness and lost! Israel never saw that goat again!

Their sins had been removed for another year.

But our salvation is "borne away" *"in His own body on the tree"* (1 Pet. 2:24), never to return.

The prophet Isaiah, writing Israel's redemption song, tells us that *"God will divide him a portion with the great and he shall divide the spoil with the strong, because he hath poured out his soul unto death"* —the fulfilment of the sacrificial goat—*"and was numbered with the transgressors and bore* [away] *the sins of many"*—the fulfilment of the scapegoat (Isa. 53:12).

We had a brother in our fellowship, now with the Lord, who said three things about our sins:

THEY ARE OUT OF HIS REACH

1. *"As far as the east is from the west, so far hath he removed our transgression from us"* (Ps. 103:12).

THEY ARE OUT OF HIS SIGHT

2. *" God has cast all our sins behind His back"* (Isa. 38:17).

THEY ARE OUT OF HIS MIND

3. *"Their sins and iniquities will I remember no more"* (Heb. 10:17).

Praise God from whom all blessings flow!

Let us think now about the "redeemer". He must have two basic qualifications, he must be willing to redeem and he must be able to redeem.

In the story of Ruth, the nearest of kin said, *"I will redeem it."*

141

He was willing, until he realized that the redemption included taking Ruth as his wife. He was neither willing nor able to do this. His commitments would not permit it. Our Kinsman Redeemer was both willing and able. He was one hundred percent committed! Hebrews 7:25 confirms that, " *He is able to save to the uttermost all that come unto God by Him, seeing He ever liveth to make intercession for them.*"

Not only does He save us daily from the power of sin, in the coming day He will save us from the very presence of sin, claiming His purchased possession (Eph. 1:14). The basic idea of this rather technical expression is "to claim for oneself." It has to do with us being God's inheritance. It is true that, as His children, we have an inheritance in Him, but it takes some mind-stretching that He has procured us for His inheritance!

Complete redemption means glory. Our souls and our spirits are presently the recipients of God's saving grace. When the Lord Jesus, our Redeemer, returns, our physical bodies will receive full and final salvation (Rom. 8:23). They will be resurrected and refashioned in all respects like His body of glory (1 Cor. 15).

To illustrate the truth of redemption, the story is told of a slave owner who one day visited the market looking for a suitable purchase. When we put this into the context of our redemption, it reminds us of the Redeemer's entry into the world—the place where men and woman are held *"captive by the devil at his will"*(2 Tim. 2:26). The ransom price was His own blood. In truth, however, the ransom price was not paid to the slave owner—the god of this world. No, it was paid to the Great Owner, the Creator of the universe, whose claim to the ownership of mankind had been usurped. Heaven was satisfied with the purchase money! Christ our Lord, resurrected in the power of an indestructible life, is the first fruits of a harvest of released captives.

Our illustration tells us that, once purchased, the slave is taken out of the market. His new owner treats him with unexpected kindness and generosity. He actually takes him right into his mansion, where he gives him the privileges normally accorded to children in the family.

The redemption of the cross proclaims that we are no longer under the domination of sin. Christ is our master, while sin has been relegated to being a tenant living in us. We are under new management! Scripture asserts that *"whom the Son makes free, is free indeed"* (John 8:36). The erstwhile slave, now in residence in his new home, will never be back in the slave market again.

VI.

"In whom we have redemption through His blood, the forgiveness of sins, according to the riches of His grace, wherein He hath abounded towards us in all wisdom and prudence" (Eph. 1:7-8).

"The blood of Jesus Christ, God's Son, cleanses us from all sin…. If we confess our sins, He is faithful and just to forgive us our sins and to cleanse us from all unrighteousness" (1 John 1:7-9).

May I ask you a question? *"The forgiveness of sins."* What sins? Those I committed before I believed?

Yes, you say, I believe that!

But what of all the sins since I believed, are they forgiven? What about the sins of thought, word and deed today, are they forgiven?

And what of the sins of the future? It is not what our opinion that counts, but what God's word says.

As I write, I see in my mind's eye a picture in an office in Bucharest, Romania. It is of a tranquil lake surrounded by mountains. A notice stands out of the lake. On it there are two Romanian words written. As I puzzle to know their meaning, my attention is drawn to text at the bottom:

"Thou wilt cast their sins into the depth of the sea" (Mic. 7:19).

I now understand. The notice reads:

NO FISHING!

And God's grace has given this total forgiveness to us in *"all wisdom and prudence."*

In all wisdom—Wisdom was a favourite word with the Greeks of New Testament times. For them it conjured up cleverness, skills in handicrafts, intelligence, philosophy and other associated ideas.

When the Bible writers use the word 'wisdom' in relation to God, they were speaking about intelligence associated with goodness—a wisdom that far transcends all human or extra-terrestrial intelligences.

If wisdom is Divine intelligence, prudence is putting that heavenly wisdom into effect, in order to bring the person receiving it to a greater understanding of what God is doing.

VII.

"In whom ye also trusted, after that ye heard the word of truth, the gospel of your salvation: In whom also after that ye believed, ye were sealed with the Holy Spirit of promise, which is the earnest of our inheritance until the redemption of the purchased possession, unto the praise of His glory" (Eph. 1:13-14).

The period of time between our purchase and our ultimate glorification is taken care of by the Holy Spirit. He is not only with us but in us. This is in fulfilment of our Redeemer's promise: *"I will pray the Father, and He will send you **another**... He dwelleth with you and shall be in you"* (John 14:6).

The personal pronoun "He" is used signifying that the Spirit is a Divine Person. This is emphasised by the use of the word "another"—in the original language this means another of the same kind. We ask, Who is Jesus? He is God; so we have here all three persons of the Godhead in unity. The Spirit, therefore, is in each of us from the moment we trust Christ. He is called the "earnest of our inheritance." The earnest is described as deposit money, deposited by the purchaser in pledge of full payment.

My grandmother, as a girl of seventeen, went into domestic service in Glasgow. On entry she was paid one shilling which was the guarantee, that if she worked to please her mistress, she would be paid the balance of her wages at the end of six months. This advance was called the "earls". I have often wondered if the word was a corruption of "earnest".

The final key thought also reinforces the guarantee, when the apostle refers to *"being sealed with the holy Spirit of **promise"*** God's word cannot be broken. His word is His bond.

The sealing of the Spirit concludes the apostle's catalogue of blessings! To help us understand what is in mind, some of us are old enough to remember the way that letters and postal packages were sealed by the Post Office. The knots in the string that tied up the envelope or package were covered in hot sealing wax. The sealing denoted that an extra charge had been paid to secure safe arrival at the stated destination. The Postal authorities had undertaken ownership and security of the goods until delivery.

What a comforting thought in the midst of life's uncertainties! Our Redeemer has bought us to possess us as His property with a guarantee of safe arrival in the "house of many mansions."

And, as if to underscore the wonder of all that we have been told in this first part of the apostle's letter to the church at Ephesus, we conclude this study with the opening words of Chapter 2: *"And **you** hath he quickened* [made to live] *who were **dead in trespasses and sins"***!

To come from where we were to where we are now and where we will be is quite beyond our comprehension.

Vindication And Validation

"Behold, He cometh with clouds; and every eye shall see Him, and they also which pierced Him: and all kindreds of the earth shall wail because of Him" (Rev. 1:7).

"...ye shall see the Son of man sitting on the right hand of power, and coming in the clouds of heaven" (Mark 14:62).

Men of the world spend fortunes trying to clear their names. There is nothing so terrible as a man dying while under suspicion or wrongful accusation. That is how the Saviour died. His accusers said, *"that deceiver said..."* (Matt. 27:63). *"He saved others: let Him save Himself, if He be the Christ, the chosen of God"* (Luke 23:35). It was plain to see that they understood the implications. They believed that there would be a Messiah, but a Messiah that ended up on a cross must be a fraud.

The chief priests protested to Pilate because they did not believe his claim to be the King of the Jews. They said, *"Write not, the king of the Jews; but that He said, 'I am the king of the Jews'"* (John 10:21).

The last time the nation of Israel saw Him, He was impaled in shame on a tree!

What a shock it will be to the national conscience, when their Messiah enters Jerusalem via the Mount of Olives, bearing the marks of Golgotha's crucifixion. The prophet Zechariah says, that *"They will look upon Him whom they have pierced and mourn for Him as a man mourns for his only son."* And the thrice spoken words from the excellent glory will be seen to be true, ***"This is My beloved Son in whom I am well pleased."***

And what about the validation of His claims?

Is He the Son of Man? **Yes!**

Is He King? **Yes!** *"The Lord shall be king over all the earth"* (Zech. 14:9).

Is He truly the Messiah, the anointed of Jehovah? **Yes!** And when Israel sees Him, they will cry out, *"Surely He hath borne our griefs, and carried our sorrows"* (Isa. 53:4).

Two reasons, therefore, why the Lord Jesus must and will return:

The vindication of His name.
The validation of His claims.

Words Of Wisdom

"Trust in the Lord with all your heart and lean not on your own understanding. In all your ways acknowledge Him and He shall direct your paths. Honour the Lord with the first fruits of all your increase" (Prov. 3:5-10).

Wise king Solomon has left us three excellent and timely messages:

1. **"Trust** in the Lord with **all** your heart."

Keep your heart with **all** diligence for out of it are.

This has to do with our **affections**.

In Proverbs 4:23 we are told to *"keep your heart with all diligence for out of it are the issues of life"*. We are listening here to something that touches the fundamentals of our very existence. It is about how we are and what we are inwardly. In this, the day that God has exhibited to us His love and grace, our life for Him must show, with gratitude, that same affection and implicit trust. This is the starting place on a road that leads to a fulfilled life.

Do not trust to luck or chance

Do not live on a wing and a prayer.

Do not look to the stars.

Do not even trust your wits.

2. **Acknowledge** the Lord in **all** your **ways.**

This has to do with our **activities**.

In the hustle and bustle of everyday life, is there time for consulting the Lord? It never occurs to the man in the street to consult Him. But if we profess to have put our faith in Him for personal forgiveness and salvation, He wants us to confide in Him. It may not minimise or prevent the problems of life, but we will have the contentment of knowing that in the eyes and heart of an all knowing God, He is working out His purposes for our good.

3. Honour the Lord with **all** your **substance**.

This has to do with your **assets**.

In all the things that God has given, and will yet give to us, we must honour—be accountable to—Him. We must ensure that we recognize that the source of all that we are and have comes from God Himself, be it little or much. This will lead us to have a **big** heart for others in need, both in the world and in the *"household of faith."* The Apostle Paul reminds us in 2 Corinthians 9:7 that *"God loves a cheerful giver."* He says we must not give *"grudgingly or of necessity."* He also reminds us in 1 Corinthians 16:1 to *"lay by us....as God has prospered us"* The royal rule is, He gets **first** not **last**!

The Land and People of Israel
by Drew Craig

The ominous storm clouds and sunshine on the horizon of the picture on the front cover afford a vivid illustration of the nation of ISRAEL today. However the contents of this little booklet concentrate more on the future sunshine that the Nation can look forward to.

When this takes place it will initiate a new era for ISRAEL as a nation. There is much about the coming events referred to by the author that are difficult to fully understand because as the Aplostle says "...we see through a glass, darkly" (1 Cor. 13:12). However the chief objective is to stimulate a greater interest in and an increasing awareness of the realities that are soon to dawn on a troubled world.

ISBN: 9-781897-117811

B-7811

64 pages

CAN: $9.99

US: $8.99

CPSIA information can be obtained at www.ICGtesting.com
Printed in the USA
BVOW03s0944291113

337565BV00009B/171/P